interchange

English for international communication

Jack C. Richards

3

Lab Guide

CAMBRIDGE
UNIVERSITY PRESS

Published by the Press Syndicate of the University of Cambridge
The Pitt Building, Trumpington Street, Cambridge CB2 1RP
40 West 20th Street, New York, NY 10011-4211, USA
10 Stamford Road, Oakleigh, Melbourne 3166, Australia

© Cambridge University Press 1992

First published 1992
Second printing 1993

Printed in the United States of America

ISBN 0 521 42221 3 Lab Cassettes Set Three
ISBN 0 521 42222 1 Lab Guide Three
ISBN 0 521 37684 X Student's Book Three
ISBN 0 521 37686 6 Workbook Three
ISBN 0 521 37685 8 Teacher's Manual Three
ISBN 0 521 37536 3 Class Cassette Three
ISBN 0 521 37537 1 Student Cassette Three

Layout and design studio: R. B. Johnson Associates

Contents

	Part 1 (directions only)	Part 2 (partial script)	Part 3 (complete script)

Introduction

Interchange Lab Cassettes

For each level of *Interchange* there is a set of four Lab Cassettes, accompanied by a Lab Guide. The Lab Cassettes contain practice exercises that supplement each unit of the Student's Book. The Lab Cassettes can be used in the language laboratory, in the classroom, or at home by the student who wants extra practice outside of class. The Lab Cassettes provide additional learning support for the student in the following ways:

- They give additional practice of the grammar patterns and functions in each unit of the Student's Book.
- They provide extra practice of the vocabulary and pronunciation patterns in the Student's Book.
- They provide further opportunities to practice some of the Conversations from the Student's Book.
- They further develop students' listening comprehension skills.

The exercises on the Lab Cassettes therefore help students develop the foundations for oral fluency.

Types of exercises on the Lab Cassettes

Each unit on the Lab Cassettes corresponds to the same unit in the Student's Book (although there are no review units on the Lab Cassettes). A variety of exercise types is used, ranging from simple listen-and-repeat tasks to more interactive activities. The exercises typically present students with a cue that requires a response, which students record on their cassette or lab recorder. Then students hear the answer modeled on the cassette for comparison. Students are not required to make written responses.

Although some of the lab exercises provide further opportunities to practice material introduced in the Student's Book, some exercises are extension activities, building on and developing vocabulary, functions, or grammar points from the Student's Book. The order of exercises *in general* follows the sequence of teaching points in the Student's Book. Hence, each unit on the Lab Cassettes complements the corresponding unit in the Student's Book as a whole. For this reason, it is best to use the Lab Cassette activities when you have finished (or have almost finished) a unit in the Student's Book.

How an exercise is presented on the Lab Cassettes

An exercise typically has the following format. The announcer gives the instructions:

Unit 1, Exercise 1
You will hear a word, then a statement about Jack, like this:
- easygoing
- Jack always worries about things and gets angry easily.

Then you will hear a question, like this:
- Is Jack easygoing?

Answer the question, like this:
- No, he isn't easygoing.

The boldface type indicates that this is the answer that the student should give. The instructions are then repeated again, or a second example is given:

Listen to another example:
- independent
- Jack likes to decide things for himself. He doesn't usually ask other people for help or advice.
- Is Jack independent?*
- Yes, he's independent.

Ready.

Students make their response when they hear the tone (indicated by an asterisk in the script). There is ample time on the cassette for the students to answer, so it is not necessary to pause the tape. When the announcer says "Ready," the exercise begins, like this:

1. sociable
   - Maria doesn't go out much. She doesn't really enjoy meeting people or making new friends.
   - Is Maria sociable?*

[The student responds. There is ample time on the cassette.]
– No, she isn't sociable.
[The answer is modeled on the cassette to give students immediate feedback.]

When to use the Lab Guide

The Lab Guide is intended as a teacher reference and learner resource. Although the goal is for students to do the exercises on the Lab Cassettes by listening only, students may initially need print support. Therefore, the Lab Guide offers different alternatives:

– **Part 1** of the Lab Guide presents the *directions only* to each exercise. These can be photocopied by the teacher for student reference or displayed on an overhead transparency if necessary.
– **Part 2** of the Lab Guide is for students who need even more support. It presents the complete script for each exercise with a dotted line to indicate where the answer goes. Again, scripts from this part may be photocopied as necessary for student reference. Once students are comfortable with the exercises, however, they should try the exercises using only the written directions from Part 1. Eventually they should be able to do the exercises only by listening, without using print support.
– **Part 3** presents the complete script, with answers indicated in boldface type to aid in checking answers. Teachers can also use this section to preview material.

Thus the Lab Guide offers great flexibility, allowing each student in the class to work at his or her own level of ability and to progress accordingly.

How to use the Lab Cassettes

Since the Lab Cassettes correspond to the Student's Book, it is assumed that students will already be familiar with the words and structures in the exercises. There are 6–7 exercises per unit in Level 3, and entire units average around 15 minutes each in length.

In the language laboratory

■ Students do not need to bring their Student's Books to the laboratory in order to do the Lab Cassette exercises.
■ Either in class or in the lab, the teacher should introduce the lab exercises by telling students which exercises they will be doing. If necessary, the teacher can go over the instructions to the exercises ahead of time to make sure students understand what to do.

■ The very first time students use the Lab Cassettes, it may be helpful to do one entire exercise as a class (see "How an Exercise Is Presented on the Lab Cassettes" on page v). This will familiarize them with the general exercise format.

■ It is not necessary for students to make notes or write while doing the exercises – in fact, it will prevent them from listening effectively.

■ If the lab allows it, students should record their responses. After they have completed their assignment, they can go back and check their responses.

■ Limit the amount of time that students spend doing the lab exercises to 15–20 minutes per session. Students are likely to get greater benefits from the exercises if they spend shorter periods of time doing them.

In the classroom

The Lab Cassettes may also be used in the classroom as a follow-up to a unit or part of a unit. Here are some suggested procedures for the teacher:

■ Play the instructions to an exercise for the class. Check that students understand what to do. If necessary, write the instructions (or just the example) on the board, or put them on an overhead transparency.

■ Students can make responses during the exercise as a class, or individually by taking turns around the class.

■ Optional: After completing an exercise, have students extend the exercise by providing further cues for other students in the class to respond to (or you can provide further cues yourself).

For self-study

Students who want extra practice outside the classroom can use the Lab Cassettes for self-study.

■ If the student has access to two tape recorders, the Lab Cassette can be played on one recorder, and the other recorder can be used for recording responses. The student or the teacher can then check the responses.

Part 1

Part 1 contains *only the directions* to each exercise. Read the directions as you listen to the recording. Then do the exercises.

Unit 1 That's what friends are for

Unit 1, Exercise 1

You will hear a word, then a statement about Jack, like this:
– easygoing
– Jack always worries about things and gets angry easily.

Then you will hear a question, like this:
– Is Jack easygoing?

Answer the question, like this:
– **No, he isn't easy going.**

Listen to another example:
– independent
– Jack likes to decide things for himself. He doesn't usually ask other people for help or advice.
– Is Jack independent?*
– **Yes, he's independent.**

Ready.

Unit 1, Exercise 2

You are looking for a roommate. Listen to people talking about possible roommates, like this:
– You wouldn't like Maria. She's too quiet.

Respond like this:
– **Oh, that doesn't matter. I like people who are quiet.**

Listen to another example.
– You wouldn't want John. He's too independent.*
– **Oh, that doesn't matter. I like people who are independent.**

Ready.

Unit 1, Exercise 3

[*Note:* This conversation is on page 2 of the Student's Book.]

Listen to this conversation.

Now repeat each sentence. Ready.

Unit 1, Exercise 4

Listen to people describe things they don't like. Answer with "I can't stand them either" or "I don't like them either," like this:
– I can't stand people who are late.*
– **I can't stand them either.**

– I don't like people who are moody.*
– **I don't like them either.**

Ready.

Unit 1, Exercise 5

Listen to a description of different people, like this:
– Mary really wants to be a successful business-person. She plans to open a business of her own in two years and be a millionaire by the time she's 30.

Then choose the best word to describe the person's personality, like this:
– Is Mary ambitious or competitive?*
– **She's ambitious.**

Listen to another example.
– Ted loves going out to meet people. He doesn't like to stay at home and be alone.
– Is Ted sociable or shy?*
– **He's sociable.**

Ready.

Unit 1, Exercise 6

You will hear a question and a response, like this:
MAN: When did your family move to England?
WOMAN: When I was in primary school.

Respond like this:
– **Her family moved to England when she was in primary school.**

Listen to another example.
WOMAN: When did you learn Spanish?
MAN: While I was in college.*
– **He learned Spanish while he was in college.**

Ready.

1

Unit 2   On the job

Unit 2, Exercise 1

Listen to a question comparing two professions.
Answer with the second one, like this:
– Who do you think is better paid: a teacher or
  a lawyer?*
– **I think a lawyer is better paid than a
  teacher.**

Listen to another example.
– Which is more interesting: being an
  accountant or a teacher?*
– **I think being a teacher is more
  interesting than being an accountant.**

Ready.

Unit 2, Exercise 2

Listen to a phrase about a job. Does it describe
the best or the worst thing about a job?
Respond like this:
– the regular hours*
– **The best thing about the job is the
  regular hours.**

– the low salary*
– **The worst thing about the job is the low
  salary.**

Ready.

Unit 2, Exercise 3

[*Note:* This conversation is on page 11 of the
Student's Book.]

Listen to this conversation.

Now repeat each sentence. Ready.

Unit 2, Exercise 4

Listen to a question about abilities, like this:
– How well do you speak French?

Reply like this:
– **I speak French pretty well.**

Listen to another example.
– How well do you type?*
– **I type pretty well.**

Ready.

Unit 2, Exercise 5

Respond to the questions you hear like this:
– How well do you speak German?*
– **I can't speak German very well.**

– How well can you translate?*
– **I can't translate very well.**

Ready.

Unit 2, Exercise 6

Listen to a question about jobs, like this:
– What kind of job are you looking for?

Then you will hear a phrase, like this:
– meet people

Answer like this:
– **I'd like a job where I can meet people.**

Listen again.
– What kind of job are you looking for?
– work with computers*
– **I'd like a job where I can work with
  computers.**

Ready.

Unit 2, Exercise 7

You will hear two words or phrases, like this:
– French, Spanish

Make a statement like this:
– **I'm good at French, but I'm not very
  good at Spanish.**

Listen to another example.
– writing, speaking in public*
– **I'm good at writing, but I'm not very
  good at speaking in public.**

Ready.

Unit 3   Destinations

Unit 3, Exercise 1

You will hear statements about different places. Listen and repeat. Ready.

Unit 3, Exercise 2

Listen to a phrase. Then use it in a sentence, like this:
- the weather*
- **Tell me about the weather in your hometown.**

Then you will hear a reply. Listen to another example.
- industry*
- **Tell me about industry in your hometown.**
- Oh, there isn't much industry.

Ready.

Unit 3, Exercise 3

Listen to questions about the weather, like this:
- Do you get much snow in the winter?

If you hear "No," reply like this:
- **No, we don't get much snow in the winter.**

If you hear "Yes," reply like this:
- **Yes, we get a lot of snow in the winter.**

Here are two examples.
- Do you get much snow in the winter? No.*
- **No, we don't get much snow in the winter.**

- Is there much humidity in the summer? Yes.*
- **Yes, there's a lot of humidity in the summer.**

Ready.

Unit 3, Exercise 4

[*Note:* This conversation is on page 16 of the Student's Book.]

Listen to this conversation.

Now listen and repeat each sentence. Ready.

Unit 3, Exercise 5

You will hear a question about two things, like this:
- Are there many shops and restaurants around here?

Reply like this:
- **There are plenty of shops, but there aren't many restaurants.**

Listen to another example.
- Are there many guesthouses and hotels in your hometown?*
- **There are plenty of guesthouses, but there aren't many hotels.**

Ready.

Unit 3, Exercise 6

Listen to people describing places they visited. Do they have a positive or negative opinion of each place? Say "positive" or "negative." Listen to an example.
- It's a crowded place. There are too many people living there, and there aren't any parks or open spaces.*
- **Negative.**

Listen to another example.
- It's a charming little town. It has lots of interesting shops on the main street, and the weather is very pleasant.*
- **Positive.**

Ready.

Unit 3, Exercise 7

Listen to two people talking about different places. Then choose the topic they were talking about. Listen to an example.
- What is the topic: the people or the climate?
- Yes, it's pretty hot, and very humid. I prefer it in the winter. It's much cooler then.
- What is the topic: the people or the climate?*
- **The climate.**

Ready.

Unit 4 What a story!

Unit 4, Exercise 1

Listen to a statement about an event, followed by a Wh-word, like this:
– There was a bank robbery downtown this morning.
– Where.

Ask a question with the Wh-word, like this:
– **_Where_ was the bank robbery?**

Then you will hear a reply. Listen to another example.
– There was a traffic accident on the freeway last night.
– When.*
– **_When_ was the traffic accident?**
– Last night, around 10.

Ready.

Unit 4, Exercise 2

Listen to people talking about news events. What topic are they talking about? Listen to an example, like this:
– What is the topic: an art exhibition or a concert?
– It was very crowded. There were lots of interesting paintings on display. And some of the artists were there to answer questions about their paintings.
– What is the topic: an art exhibition or a concert?*
– **An art exhibition.**

Ready.

Unit 4, Exercise 3

Reply to each question about a news event like this:
– Did you hear about the fire downtown?*
– **No, I didn't know there was a fire downtown.**

Ready.

Unit 4, Exercise 4

Listen to people describe things that happened to them. Respond like this:
– Someone ran into my car!*
– **Someone ran into your car? When did that happen?**

Then you will hear a reply, like this:
– This morning.

Respond like this:
– **That's too bad.**

Listen to another example.
– I got fired from my job.*
– **You got fired from your job? When did that happen?**
– Yesterday.*
– **That's too bad.**

Ready.

Unit 4, Exercise 5

[*Note:* This conversation is on page 25 of the Student's Book.]

Listen to this conversation.

Now repeat each sentence. Ready.

Unit 4, Exercise 6

Answer these questions about a traffic accident with the second choice, like this:
– Was your friend driving or were you driving the car?*
– **I was driving the car.**

Ready.

Unit 4, Exercise 7

Listen to a statement, like this:
– Something interesting happened while I was driving to work today.

Ask what happened, like this:
– **Really? What happened while you were driving to work?**

Then you will hear a response. Listen to another example.
– Something interesting happened while I was shopping.*
– **Really? What happened while you were shopping?**
– I saw someone shoplifting.

Ready.

Unit 5   Could you do me a favor?

Unit 5, Exercise 1

Make a request using "Could you" and "Please," like this:
– Open the window.*
– **Could you open the window, please?**

Then you will hear a reply. Listen to another example.
– Pass me that book.*
– **Could you pass me that book, please?**
– Yes, here you are.

Ready.

Unit 5, Exercise 2

Make a request using "Would you mind," like this:
– Close the window.*
– **Would you mind closing the window?**

Then listen to the reply. Listen to another example.
– Type this letter for me.*
– **Would you mind typing this letter for me?**
– Sorry, I can't type.

Ready.

Unit 5, Exercise 3

Listen to people making requests. Did the second speaker agree or refuse? Listen to this example.
A: I wonder if I could borrow your car on Sunday.
B: Well, actually, I have to take my sister to the airport. Sorry.
– Did the second speaker agree or refuse?*
– **Refuse.**

Ready.

Unit 5, Exercise 4

Listen to people ask you to do something. Politely refuse, like this:
– I wonder if you'd mind taking me to the airport tonight.*
– **Oh, I'm sorry. I can't take you to the airport tonight.**

Ready.

Unit 5, Exercise 5

[*Note:* This conversation is on page 31 of the Student's Book.]

Listen to this conversation.

Now repeat each sentence. Ready.

Unit 5, Exercise 6

Ask someone to give messages to Sue, like this:
– Jack's having a party tonight.*
– **Could you tell Sue that Jack's having a party tonight?**

Listen to another example.
– There's a tennis game on Saturday.*
– **Could you tell Sue that there's a tennis game on Saturday?**

Ready.

Unit 6   Comparatively speaking

Unit 6, Exercise 1

Answer the questions with the second choice, like this:
- Would you rather learn the piano or the guitar?*
- **I'd rather learn the guitar.**

- Would you rather live in a house or an apartment?*
- **I'd rather live in an apartment.**

Ready.

Unit 6, Exercise 2

Ask a question with "Would rather," like this:
- work outdoors or indoors*
- **Would you rather work outdoors or indoors?**

Then you will hear a reply. Listen to another example.
- listen to classical music or pop music*
- **Would you rather listen to classical music or pop music?**
- Oh, I prefer classical music.

Ready.

Unit 6, Exercise 3

Answer each question with the second choice. Then ask a follow-up question, like this:
- Do you prefer studying part-time or full-time?*
- **I prefer studying full-time. How about you?**

Then you will hear a response. Listen to another example.
- Do you prefer reading or watching TV?*
- **I prefer watching TV. How about you?**
- Oh, I prefer reading.

Ready.

Unit 6, Exercise 4

[*Note:* This conversation is on page 34 of the Student's Book.]

Listen to this conversation.

Now repeat each sentence. Ready.

Unit 6, Exercise 5

Answer the questions with the first choice. Then ask a follow-up question, like this:
- Is your sister teaching at an elementary school or a secondary school?*
- **She's teaching at an elementary school. Where is your sister teaching?**

Then you will hear a response. Listen to another example.
- Do you go to a public school or a private school?*
- **I go to a public school. Where do you go?**
- I go to a public school too.

Ready.

Unit 6, Exercise 6

Answer the questions like this:
- Do a lot of students go to school until they're 16 here?*
- **Yes, in fact most students go to school until they're 16 here.**

- Do a lot of colleges teach French?*
- **Yes, in fact most colleges teach French.**

Ready.

Unit 6, Exercise 7

Listen to statements about education. Ask for clarification by repeating each statement, like this:
- Very few schools teach Korean.*
- **Did you say that very few schools teach Korean?**

Then you will hear a reply. Listen to another example.
- Neither teachers nor students wear uniforms.*
- **Did you say that neither teachers nor students wear uniforms?**
- That's right.

Ready.

Unit 7 Don't drink the water

Unit 7, Exercise 1

Practice saying consonant clusters with /s/.
Listen and repeat. Ready.

Unit 7, Exercise 2

Listen to a phrase, like this:
– to see old cities

Use it to complete this sentence:
– Many people visit Europe.

Listen to two examples:
– to see old cities*
– **Many people visit Europe to see old cities.**

– to shop*
– **Many people visit Europe to shop.**

Ready.

Unit 7, Exercise 3

Report what each person says, like this:
WOMAN: I'm going to Spain. I want to learn Spanish.*
– **She's going to Spain so she can learn Spanish.**

MAN: I'm going to London. I want to find a job there.*
– **He's going to London so he can find a job there.**

Ready.

Unit 7, Exercise 4

[*Note:* This conversation is on page 42 of the Student's Book.]

Listen to this conversation.

Now repeat each sentence. Ready.

Unit 7, Exercise 5

Report each person's reasons with "because of," like this:
WOMAN: I don't like Hong Kong. There's too much pollution.*
– **She doesn't like Hong Kong because of the pollution.**

MAN: I like living in Italy. I really love the food.*

– He likes living in Italy because of the food.

Ready.

Unit 7, Exercise 6

Listen to people talk about different places. They say some good points and *one* problem. What problem do they mention? Listen to an example:
WOMAN: I loved my vacation in Thailand. The beaches were fantastic and the hotels were reasonably priced. Unfortunately it was very crowded because it was tourist season.
– What problem does she mention?*
– **It was very crowded.**

Listen to another example.
MAN: I enjoyed my trip a lot. The city had excellent museums, and I enjoyed the theater too. There was only one drawback: It wasn't safe at night. I had to be careful.
– What problem does he mention?*
– **It wasn't safe at night.**

Ready.

Unit 7, Exercise 7

You are talking to someone about customs in their country. Ask questions with "What happens when . . . " like this:
– You are invited to someone's house for dinner.*
– **What happens when you are invited to someone's house for dinner?**

Then you will hear a reply. Listen to another example.
– You meet someone for the first time.*
– **What happens when you meet someone for the first time?**
– Oh, you generally shake hands.

Ready.

Unit 8   Getting things done

Unit 8, Exercise 1

Ask where you can get things done, like this:
- a passport photo taken*
- **Do you know where I could get a passport photo taken?**

Then you will hear a reply. Listen to another example.
- my hair cut*
- **Do you know where I could get my hair cut?**
- Sure. There's a barber down the street, at the corner.

Ready.

Unit 8, Exercise 2

Listen to a guest at a hotel say things that need to be done, like this:
- I need to have these shoes repaired.

You are the hotel clerk. Reply like this:
- **Oh, I'll have them repaired for you.**

Listen to another example.
- I need to have this suit cleaned.*
- **Oh, I'll have it cleaned for you.**

Ready.

Unit 8, Exercise 3

Practice the sounds /s/ and /sh/. Listen and repeat these sentences. Ready.

Unit 8, Exercise 4

[*Note:* This conversation is on page 51 of the Student's Book.]

Listen to this conversation.

Now repeat each sentence. Ready.

Unit 8, Exercise 5

Listen to a phrase like this:
- hear live music

Ask a question using "Where's a good place to," like this:
- hear live music*
- **Where's a good place to hear live music?**

Listen to the reply, and then repeat the location and thank the speaker, like this:

- At the disco.*
- **At the disco? OK, thanks.**

Listen to the whole example again.
- hear live music*
- **Where's a good place to hear live music?**
- At the disco.*
- **At the disco? OK, thanks.**

Listen to another example.
- buy fresh seafood*
- **Where's a good place to buy fresh seafood?**
- At the fish market downtown.*
- **At the fish market downtown? OK, thanks.**

Ready.

Unit 8, Exercise 6

Listen to a question. Then you will hear someone describing a place. Answer the question, like this:
- What is she describing: a disco, a library, or a bank?
- FEMALE: It's always busy. A lot of tourists go there to change traveler's checks. And of course it's in the business district, so a lot of businesses have accounts there. But the service is quick and efficient, and the tellers are very friendly.
- What is she describing: a disco, a library, or a bank?*
- **A bank.**

Ready.

Unit 8, Exercise 7

Answer questions about different places, like this:
- Is the nightclub noisy?*
- **No, I like it because it's not so noisy.**

- Is the beach crowded?*
- **No, I like it because it's not so crowded.**

Ready.

Unit 9 Is that a fact?

Unit 9, Exercise 1

You will hear four numbers. What year do they describe? Listen and say the year, like this:
– 1, 9, 2, 3*
– **The year nineteen twenty-three.**
– 1, 5, 0, 0*
– **The year fifteen hundred.**

Ready.

Unit 9, Exercise 2

You will hear an event like this:
– the first flight in a jumbo jet

Ask a question with "When was . . . ," like this:
– **When was the first flight in a jumbo jet?**

Then you will hear a reply. Listen to another example.
– the first satellite launched*
– **When was the first satellite launched?**
– In the late fifties, I believe.

Ready.

Unit 9, Exercise 3

Listen to a statement about a past event, like this:
– World War One began.

Ask a question with "When did," like this:
– **When did World War One begin?**

Then you will hear the answer. Listen to another example.
– World War Two ended.*
– **When did World War Two end?**
– In 1945.

Ready.

Unit 9, Exercise 4

[*Note:* This conversation is on page 57 of the Student's Book.]

Listen to this conversation.

Now listen and repeat each sentence. Ready.

Unit 9, Exercise 5

Listen to a phrase. Then ask questions about what will happen in five years, like this:
– living in the same place*
– **Do you think you'll be living in the same place in five years?**

Then you will hear a reply. Listen to another example.
– have the same friends*
– **Do you think you'll have the same friends in five years?**
– No, I'll probably have lots of new friends in five years.

Ready.

Unit 9, Exercise 6

Listen to predictions about the year 2050. Disagree by making a negative statement, like this:
– People will be living on the moon.*
– **Oh, I don't think people will be living on the moon.**

– They will have discovered a cure for cancer.*
– **Oh, I don't think they will have discovered a cure for cancer.**

Ready.

Unit 10   There's no place like home

Unit 10, Exercise 1

Reply to questions about household chores, like this:
- Do you like washing dishes?*
- **No, I can't stand washing dishes. How about you?**

Then you will hear a reply. Listen to another example.
- Do you like vacuuming?*
- **No, I can't stand vacuuming. How about you?**
- I can't stand it either.

Ready.

Unit 10, Exercise 2

Answer questions about a house or an apartment, like this:
- Does it have a kitchen and a laundry room?*
- **It has a kitchen, but it doesn't have a laundry room.**

- Does it have a patio and a yard?*
- **It has a patio, but it doesn't have a yard.**

Ready.

Unit 10, Exercise 3

Answer the questions you hear about a town or neighborhood, like this:
- Is there a good bus system and a subway?*
- **Yes, there's a good bus system as well as a subway.**

- Is there a shopping mall and a market?*
- **Yes, there's a shopping mall as well as a market.**

Ready.

Unit 10, Exercise 4

[*Note:* This conversation is on page 62 of the Student's Book.]

Listen to this conversation.

Now repeat each sentence. Ready.

Unit 10, Exercise 5

Answer questions about a neighborhood, like this:
- Is there a shopping mall and a department store?*
- **There's no shopping mall, although there's a department store.**

- Is there a movie theater and a good video store?*
- **There's no movie theater, although there's a good video store.**

Ready.

Unit 10, Exercise 6

Listen to people talking to their apartment manager about problems in their apartment. Reply with the second choice, like this:
- What's the problem? Is it the bedroom fan or the kitchen fan?*
- **It's the *kitchen* fan.**

Pay attention to stress. Listen to another example.
- What's the problem? Is it the bathroom window or the bedroom window?*
- **It's the *bedroom* window.**

Ready.

Unit 10, Exercise 7

Listen to people talking about a problem with something in their apartment. Listen and say what they are talking about, like this.
- Is she talking about the TV, the lamp, or the iron?
- WOMAN: I noticed that the room was getting darker. Then it started to make a strange buzzing sound. So I unplugged it and called a repairperson immediately.
- Is she talking about the TV, the lamp, or the iron?*
- **The lamp.**

Ready.

Unit 11 What a world we live in!

Unit 11, Exercise 1

[*Note:* This conversation is on page 68 of the Student's Book.]

Listen to this conversation.

Now repeat each sentence. Ready.

Unit 11, Exercise 2

You will hear a situation. Ask a question using "What would you do?" like this:
- Suppose you lost your job.*
- **What would you do if you lost your job?**

Then you will hear a reply. Listen to another example.
- Suppose you became president of your country.*
- **What would you do if you became president of your country?**
- I'd give everyone a job.

Ready.

Unit 11, Exercise 3

Listen to people saying what they would do if they won a million dollars. Report what they say like this:
WOMAN: What would I do? Buy a boat and sail around the world.*
- **She'd buy a boat and sail around the world.**

MAN: What would I do? Marry my childhood sweetheart.*
- **He'd marry his childhood sweetheart.**

Ready.

Unit 11, Exercise 4

Practice these sentences with plural "s." Listen and repeat. Ready.

Unit 11, Exercise 5

Listen to two people talking, like this:
A: What if the government raised taxes?
B: People would complain.

Report what they say, like this:
- **If the government raised taxes, people would complain.**

Listen to another example.
A: What if employers raised salaries?
B: People would spend more.*
- **If employers raised salaries, people would spend more.**

Ready.

Unit 11, Exercise 6

Someone is talking to you about problems in a country you have visited recently. Answer the questions like this:
- Is reducing the air pollution a problem there?*
- **Yes, reducing air pollution is a real problem.**

- Is controlling drugs a problem there?*
- **Yes, controlling drugs is a real problem.**

Ready.

Unit 11, Exercise 7

Listen to people giving opinions. What topics are they talking about? Listen to an example.
- What is she talking about: pollution, inflation, or traffic?
WOMAN: I wish we had a subway system in this city. I can't stand driving to work anymore. You know, it's only a 15-minute drive, but during rush hour it takes me an *hour.*
- What is she talking about: pollution, inflation, or traffic?*
- **Traffic.**

Ready.

Unit 12 How does it work?

Unit 12, Exercise 1

[*Note:* This conversation is on page 74 of the Student's Book.]

Listen to this conversation.

Now listen and repeat each sentence. Ready.

Unit 12, Exercise 2

Make a sentence using "that," like this:
- a machine for cleaning floors*
- **It's a machine that's used for cleaning floors.**

- a liquid for cleaning glass*
- **It's a liquid that's used for cleaning glass.**

Ready.

Unit 12, Exercise 3

Ask a question with "What's the stuff that's used" and the phrase you hear, like this:
- to stick things together*
- **What's the stuff that's used to stick things together?**

Then you will hear a reply. Listen to another example.
- to polish floors*
- **What's the stuff that's used to polish floors?**
- Oh, that's called wax.

Ready.

Unit 12, Exercise 4

Answer the questions you hear with the second choice, like this:
- Are you looking for the cassette player or the tape recorder?*
- **The *tape* recorder.**

Pay attention to stress. Listen to another example.
- Are you looking for the coffee machine or the rice cooker?*
- **The *rice* cooker.**

Ready.

Unit 12, Exercise 5

Answer each question with the first choice, like this:
- Are tires usually made of rubber or plastic?*
- **They're usually made of rubber.**

- Are windows usually made of glass or plastic?*
- **They're usually made of glass.**

Ready.

Unit 12, Exercise 6

Listen to people asking about things that need to be done and reply like this:
- Do you want me to clean the living room?*
- **Yes, it needs to be cleaned.**

- Do you want me to wash the dishes?*
- **Yes, they need to be washed.**

Ready.

Unit 12, Exercise 7

Listen to someone asking for information. Reply like this.
- Do you grow these plants inside?*
- **Yes, they're grown inside.**

- Do you clean this machine with oil?*
- **Yes, it's cleaned with oil.**

Ready.

Unit 13   That's a possibility

Unit 13, Exercise 1

Listen to how these sentences with past modals are pronounced.
"Must have":
– She must have missed the bus.

"Could have":
– She could have forgotten.

Now listen to people talking about why someone missed an appointment. Repeat the sentences. Ready.

Unit 13, Exercise 2

[*Note:* This conversation is on page 82 of the Student's Book.]

Listen to this conversation.

Now listen and repeat each sentence. Ready.

Unit 13, Exercise 3

You will hear a statement about the cause of a traffic accident, like this:
– The driver was probably drunk.

Reply with "may have," like this:
– **Yes, the driver may have been drunk.**

– The car was probably going too fast.*
– **Yes, the car may have been going too fast.**

Ready.

Unit 13, Exercise 4

A man has lost a set of keys and is trying to remember where he left them. Reply to what he says with "could have," like this:
– Maybe I left them at work.*
– **Yes, you could have left them at work.**

Ready.

Unit 13, Exercise 5

Listen to people describing things they did. Agree with them, like this:
– I found some money on the street. I took it to the police station.*
– **I would have taken it to the police station too.**
– I lost my wallet, so I put an ad in the paper.*
– **I would have put an ad in the paper too.**
Ready.

Unit 13, Exercise 6

Listen to someone talking about a job interview. Respond like this:
– Do you think I should have asked for a higher salary?*
– **No, I don't think you should have asked for a higher salary.**

– Do you think I should have said the job sounded boring?*
– **No, I don't think you should have said the job sounded boring.**

Ready.

Unit 13, Exercise 7

Listen to people talking about things they are going to do. Reply like this:
– I hate my job. I'm going to resign.*
– **I wouldn't resign if I were you.**

– My course is boring. I'm going to drop it.*
– **I wouldn't drop it if I were you.**

Ready.

Unit 14 The right stuff

Unit 14, Exercise 1

Listen and combine these statements like this:
A: What does a successful magazine need?
B: To be informative.*
– A successful magazine needs to be informative.

Listen to another example.
A: What does a successful salesperson need?
B: To be outgoing and persuasive.*
– A successful salesperson needs to be outgoing and persuasive.

Ready.

Unit 14, Exercise 2

Make sentences with "If you want to be a writer," like this:
– You have to read a lot.*
– If you want to be a writer, you have to read a lot.

– You need to have lots of ideas.*
– If you want to be a writer, you need to have lots of ideas.

Ready.

Unit 14, Exercise 3

Make sentences with "If you want to be successful in business," like this:
– You must be dynamic.*
– If you want to be successful in business, you must be dynamic.

– You need to have a lot of patience.*
– If you want to be successful in business, you need to have a lot of patience.

Ready.

Unit 14, Exercise 4

Listen to reporters on a TV news program give opinions about different things. Then answer the question, like this:
– Is the book well written?
WOMAN: The new thriller by John Clancy won't disappoint you. As usual, the story is complex and told with great skill. The characters are memorable, and the dialog is realistic.
– Is the book well written?*
– Yes, it's very well written.

Listen to another example.
– Is the restaurant in a good location?
MAN: You won't want to miss the new Chinese restaurant in the business district, which doesn't get much traffic after 5 o'clock. It looks like the restaurant will have to struggle to attract customers at night.
– Is the restaurant in a good location?*
– No, it's not in a very good location.

Ready.

Unit 14, Exercise 5

[*Note:* This conversation is on page 91 of the Student's Book.]

Listen to this conversation.

Now listen and repeat each sentence. Ready.

Unit 14, Exercise 6

Listen to people talking about different topics. What are they talking about? Listen to this example.
– What are they talking about: a TV program, a book, or a movie?
A: So what did you think?
B: I loved it! The characters were so believable.
A: Yeah, I agree. The acting was fantastic. It was definitely worth the price of admission.
B: Mm-hmm. In fact, I'm ready to go see it again!
– What are they talking about: a TV program, a book, or a movie?*
– A movie.

Ready.

Unit 15 It's a matter of opinion

Unit 15, Exercise 1

[*Note:* This conversation is on page 94 of the Student's Book.]

Listen to this conversation.

Now listen and repeat each sentence. Ready.

Unit 15, Exercise 2

Repeat each statement and add a tag question, like this:
– People are friendly around here.*
– **People are friendly around here, aren't they?**

– Parking is difficult here.*
– **Parking is difficult here, isn't it?**

Ready.

Unit 15, Exercise 3

Listen to people giving opinions. Agree with each statement like this:
– People are very friendly here, aren't they?*
– **Yes, they are.**

– The weather is awful here in the winter, isn't it?*
– **Yes, it is.**

Ready.

Unit 15, Exercise 4

Choose the word that matches the definition you hear. You will hear the definition two times. Listen to an example:
– Which word is defined: "criticize" or "contradict"?
– To point out the faults of someone or something. To point out the faults of someone or something.
– Which word was defined: "criticize" or "contradict"?*
– **Criticize.**

Ready.

Unit 15, Exercise 5

Listen to people giving opinions. Say "positive" or "negative." Ready.

Unit 15, Exercise 6

Listen to two people giving opinions about things. Do they agree or disagree?

Part 2

Part 2 contains the script for each exercise *without* the answers. When you hear a tone on the recording (shown by an asterisk * in the script), it is time to say your answer. The script has a dotted line where the answer goes.

Unit 1 That's what friends are for

Unit 1, Exercise 1

You will hear a word, then a statement about Jack, like this:
- easygoing
- Jack always worries about things and gets angry easily.

Then you will hear a question, like this:
- Is Jack easygoing?

Answer the question, like this:
- **No, he isn't easy going.**

Listen to another example:
- independent
- Jack likes to decide things for himself. He doesn't usually ask other people for help or advice.
- Is Jack independent?*
- **Yes, he's independent.**

Ready.

1 sociable
  - Maria doesn't go out much. She doesn't really enjoy meeting people or making new friends.
  - Is Maria sociable?*

. . . .

2 emotional
  - You never have to guess how Peter feels. Whether he's excited or sad, he shows his feelings very easily.
  - Is Peter emotional?*

. . . .

3 generous
  - Anne likes helping people. She often gives her friends gifts, and she enjoys spending money on other people.
  - Is Anne generous?*

. . . .

4 patient
  - Mr. Brown doesn't like waiting for anything. If you're only two minutes late for an appointment, he gets upset.
  - Is Mr. Brown patient?*

. . . .

5 proud
  - Bob talks about himself a lot. In fact, he has a very high opinion of himself.
  - Is Bob proud?*

. . . .

Unit 1, Exercise 2

You are looking for a roommate. Listen to people talking about possible roommates, like this:
- You wouldn't like Maria. She's too quiet.

Respond like this:
- **Oh, that doesn't matter. I like people who are quiet.**

Listen to another example.
- You wouldn't want John. He's too independent.*
- **Oh, that doesn't matter. I like people who are independent.**

Ready.

1 You wouldn't like Claudio. He's too serious.*

. . . .

2 You wouldn't want Sonia. She's too easygoing.*

. . . .

3 You wouldn't like Jack. He's too competitive.*

. . . .

4 You wouldn't want Sandy. She's too ambitious.*

. . . .

5 You don't want Mary. She's too quiet.*

. . . .

(Unit 1 continues on next page.)

18   *Part 2*

Unit 1, Exercise 3

[*Note:* This conversation is on page 2 of the Student's Book.]

Listen to this conversation.

DAVE: [*phone rings*] Hello?
JIM: Hi. My name's Jim Brady. I'm calling about the ad for a roommate.
DAVE: Oh, yes.
JIM: Are you still looking for someone?
DAVE: Yes, we are.
JIM: Oh, good. I'm really interested.
DAVE: Well, there are four of us, and it's a fairly small house, so we want someone who's easy to get along with.
JIM: Well, I'm pretty easygoing.
DAVE: Great! Can I ask you a few questions?

Now repeat each sentence. Ready.

Unit 1, Exercise 4

Listen to people describe things they don't like. Answer with "I can't stand them either" or "I don't like them either," like this:
– I can't stand people who are late.*
– **I can't stand them either.**

– I don't like people who are moody.*
– **I don't like them either.**

Ready.

1 I don't like people who blow smoke in my face.*
. . . .
2 I can't stand people who are selfish.*
. . . .
3 I don't like people who are lazy.*
. . . .
4 I can't stand people who are unreliable.*
. . . .
5 I can't stand people who are too emotional.*
. . . .
6 I don't like people who are impatient.*
. . . .

Unit 1, Exercise 5

Listen to a description of different people, like this:
– Mary really wants to be a successful business-person. She plans to open a business of her own in two years and be a millionaire by the time she's 30.

Then choose the best word to describe the person's personality, like this:
– Is Mary ambitious or competitive?*
– **She's ambitious.**

Listen to another example.
– Ted loves going out to meet people. He doesn't like to stay at home and be alone.
– Is Ted sociable or shy?*
– **He's sociable.**

Ready.

1 Fred is the kind of guy who always has to be the best in the class. He gets really worried if someone does better than him at something.
– Is Fred competitive or easygoing?*
. . . .
2 Anna never listens to what other people are trying to say. She always interrupts and gives her own opinion.
– Is Anna patient or impatient?*
. . . .
3 If Susan says something, you can be sure she means it. She never arrives late for an appointment, and she always does what she promises to do.
– Is Susan reliable or unreliable?*
. . . .
4 Sam is an unpredictable guy. One day he's all smiles and very friendly to people. The next day he's very quiet and doesn't want to talk to anyone.
– Is Sam sociable or moody?*
. . . .
5 Jack only thinks about himself. He hates spending money on other people, and he doesn't like helping friends, either.
– Is Jack generous or selfish?*
. . . .

Unit 1, Exercise 6

You will hear a question and a response, like this:
MAN: When did your family move to England?
WOMAN: When I was in primary school.

Respond like this:
– Her family moved to England when she was in primary school.

Listen to another example.
WOMAN: When did you learn Spanish?
MAN: While I was in college.*
– He learned Spanish while he was in college.

Ready.

1 WOMAN: When did your parents meet?
   MAN: While they were at university.*

. . . .

2 MAN: When did you learn to drive?
   WOMAN: When I was in high school.*

. . . .

3 WOMAN: When did you first start learning English?
   MAN: When I was in grade school.*

. . . .

4 MAN: When did you learn Japanese?
   WOMAN: While I was living in Japan.*

. . . .

5 WOMAN: When did you learn to cook?
   MAN: While I was working in a restaurant.

. . . .

6 WOMAN: When did you get married?
   MAN: While I was working in Brazil.*

. . . .

Unit 2   On the job

Unit 2, Exercise 1

Listen to a question comparing two professions.
Answer with the second one, like this:
– Who do you think is better paid: a teacher or
  a lawyer?*
– **I think a lawyer is better paid than a
  teacher.**

Listen to another example.
– Which is more interesting: being an
  accountant or a teacher?*
– **I think being a teacher is more
  interesting than being an accountant.**

Ready.

1 Which is more interesting: office work or
   teaching?*

   . . . .

2 Which is more challenging: being a journalist
   or a doctor?*

   . . . .

3 Who has better benefits: a taxi driver or a
   nurse?*

   . . . .

4 Which do you think is more dangerous: being
   a pilot or a police officer?*

   . . . .

5 Who do you think is better paid: a clerk or a
   construction worker?*

   . . . .

Unit 2, Exercise 2

Listen to a phrase about a job. Does it describe
the best or the worst thing about a job?
Respond like this:
– the regular hours*
– **The best thing about the job is the
  regular hours.**

– the low salary*
– **The worst thing about the job is the low
  salary.**

Ready.

1 the long vacations*

   . . . .

2 working with pleasant people*

   . . . .

3 traveling to work during rush hour*

   . . . .

4 working in a nice, quiet office*

   . . . .

5 the low salary*

   . . . .

6 being able to work at home*

   . . . .

7 getting only one week's vacation a year*

   . . . .

Unit 2, Exercise 3

[*Note:* This conversation is on page 11 of the
Student's Book.]

Listen to this conversation.

A: When did you graduate, Celia?
B: I graduated last year.
A: I see. And what have you been doing since
    then?
B: Traveling mostly. I love to travel, but now I
    think it's time for me to get a job.
A: Uh-huh. Are you good at foreign languages?
B: Yes, I think so. I speak French and German,
    and I can speak a little Russian.
A: Mmm. What kind of job are you looking for?
B: Well, I'd like to have a job where I can use
    my writing skills. I love working with
    computers and organizing information. Also,
    I'd like to work in a large office, so that I'm
    around other people.
A: OK . . . Well, I think I have the perfect job
    for you!

Now repeat each sentence. Ready.

Unit 2, Exercise 4

Listen to a question about abilities, like this:
– How well do you speak French?

Reply like this:
– **I speak French pretty well.**

Listen to another example.
– How well do you type?*
– **I type pretty well.**

Ready.

1 How well do you understand German?*

   . . . .

2 How well do you write Spanish?*

   . . . .

3 How well do you write business letters?*

   . . . .

4 How well do you work under pressure?*

   . . . .

5 How well do you understand computers?*

   . . . .

Unit 2, Exercise 5

Respond to the questions you hear like this:
- How well do you speak German?*
- **I can't speak German very well.**

- How well can you translate?*
- **I can't translate very well.**

Ready.

1 How well can you drive?*

. . . .

2 How well can you play the guitar?*

. . . .

3 How well can you play tennis?*

. . . .

4 How well can you type?*

. . . .

5 How well can you speak Spanish?*

. . . .

Unit 2, Exercise 6

Listen to a question about jobs, like this:
- What kind of job are you looking for?

Then you will hear a phrase, like this:
- meet people

Answer like this:
- **I'd like a job where I can meet people.**

Listen again.
- What kind of job are you looking for?
- work with computers*
- **I'd like a job where I can work with computers.**

Ready.

1 What kind of job would you prefer?
use my languages*

. . . .

2 What kind of job are you looking for?
travel overseas*

. . . .

3 What kind of job would you prefer?
use my writing skills*

. . . .

4 What kind of job are you hoping to find?
learn about marketing*

. . . .

5 What kind of job would you prefer?
work outdoors*

. . . .

Unit 2, Exercise 7

You will hear two words or phrases, like this:
- French, Spanish

Make a statement like this:
- **I'm good at French, but I'm not very good at Spanish.**

Listen to another example.
- writing, speaking in public*
- **I'm good at writing, but I'm not very good at speaking in public.**

Ready.

1 working on a team, managing people*

. . . .

2 writing reports, keeping deadlines*

. . . .

3 using a computer, typing*

. . . .

4 languages, math*

. . . .

5 meeting people, speaking in public*

. . . .

Unit 3   Destinations

Unit 3, Exercise 1

You will hear statements about different places.
Listen and repeat. Ready.

1 Bali is a beautiful little tropical island.*
2 Carmel is a delightful American seaside
   resort.*
3 Tokyo is a dynamic modern Japanese city.*
4 Detroit is an old American industrial city.*
5 Sorrento is a charming Italian summer
   resort.*
6 Barcelona is a delightful old Spanish city.*
7 Kensington is a fashionable London suburb.*
8 Singapore is a clean small southeast Asian
   country.*

Unit 3, Exercise 2

Listen to a phrase. Then use it in a sentence,
like this:
– the weather*
– **Tell me about the weather in your
  hometown.**

Then you will hear a reply. Listen to another
example.
– industry*
– **Tell me about industry in your
  hometown.**
– Oh, there isn't much industry.

Ready.

1 the weather*

   . . . .
   Oh, the climate is fairly mild.
2 entertainment*

   . . . .
   Well, there are plenty of theaters and
   nightclubs.
3 the cost of living*

   . . . .
   Unfortunately, it's a fairly expensive place to
   live.
4 the population*
   Tell me about the population in your
   hometown.

   . . . .
5 public transportation*

   . . . .
   Well, there's a good bus system, but no
   subway.

Unit 3, Exercise 3

Listen to questions about the weather, like this:
– Do you get much snow in the winter?

If you hear "No," reply like this:
– **No, we don't get much snow in the
  winter.**

If you hear "Yes," reply like this:
– **Yes, we get a lot of snow in the winter.**

Here are two examples.
– Do you get much snow in the winter? No.*
– **No, we don't get much snow in the
  winter.**
– Is there much humidity in the summer? Yes.*
– **Yes, there's a lot of humidity in the
  summer.**

Ready.

1 Do you get much rain in the summer? No.*
   . . . .
2 Is there much wind in the winter? Yes.*
   . . . .
3 Is there much humidity in the winter? Yes.*
   . . . .
4 Do you get much rain in the fall? Yes.*
   . . . .
5 Do you get much snow in January? No.*
   . . . .
6 Is there much sun in September? Yes.*
   . . . .
7 Do you get much snow in November? No.*
   . . . .

Unit 3, Exercise 4

[*Note:* This conversation is on page 16 of the Student's Book.]

Listen to this conversation.

A: I'm thinking about spending my vacation in southeast Asia, but I haven't decided where.
B: Oh? What kind of place are you looking for?
A: Somewhere with good weather, that's quiet and far away from the crowds.
B: Hmm, Phuket might be the place.
A: Phuket? Where's that?
B: In Thailand. It's a beautiful island with excellent beaches. I was there last summer. It's fantastic!
A: Sounds good. But what about the weather?
B: The weather is great. And there are plenty of cheap hotels along the beach.
A: It sounds just like the kind of place I'm looking for.

Now listen and repeat each sentence. Ready.

Unit 3, Exercise 5

You will hear a question about two things, like this:
– Are there many shops and restaurants around here?

Reply like this:
– **There are plenty of shops, but there aren't many restaurants.**

Listen to another example.
– Are there many guesthouses and hotels in your hometown?*
– **There are plenty of guesthouses, but there aren't many hotels.**

Ready.

1 Are there many department stores and shopping malls nearby?*
. . . .
2 Are there many offices and factories in the city?*
. . . .
3 Are there many houses and apartment buildings near the beach?*
. . . .
4 Are there many buses and taxis at the airport?*
. . . .
5 Are there many shops and markets in your hometown?*
. . . .

Unit 3, Exercise 6

Listen to people describing places they visited. Do they have a positive or negative opinion of each place? Say "positive" or "negative." Listen to an example.
– It's a crowded place. There are too many people living there, and there aren't any parks or open spaces.*
– **Negative.**

Listen to another example.
– It's a charming little town. It has lots of interesting shops on the main street, and the weather is very pleasant.*
– **Positive.**

Ready.

1 There are hardly any tourist attractions, and there's not much to do there. There aren't enough good restaurants either.*
. . . .
2 There's plenty of sightseeing, and the beaches are very clean. The people are friendly too.*
. . . .
3 There's very little poverty there and very little unemployment. In fact, the standard of living is pretty high.*
. . . .
4 There's too much pollution and there's lots of crime downtown. It's a pretty dangerous place to live.*
. . . .
5 Finding a place to stay can be pretty tricky. There are a few big hotels, but they aren't very comfortable and they are very expensive.*
. . . .

(Unit 3 continues on next page.)

Unit 3, Exercise 7

Listen to two people talking about different places. Then choose the topic they were talking about. Listen to an example.
– What is the topic: the people or the climate?
– Yes, it's pretty hot, and very humid. I prefer it in the winter. It's much cooler then.
– What is the topic: the people or the climate?*
– The climate.

Ready.

1 What is the topic: industry or tourist attractions?
 – They produce lots of things there, like cars, watches, and bicycles. So there are plenty of jobs, and unemployment is very low.
 What is the topic: industry or tourist attractions?*

. . . .

2 What is the topic: crime or shopping?
 – You'd better not go out alone at night. And be careful even during the day. Don't carry a lot of money with you or wear jewelry in public.
 What is the topic: crime or shopping?*

. . . .

3 What is the topic: housing or industry?
 – Most of the people live in high-rise apartment buildings. It's very expensive to buy a house there, and there is little public housing available.
 What is the topic: housing or industry?*

. . . .

4 What is the topic: tourist attractions or transportation?
 – There's an excellent subway system, so it's easy to get around. There are lots of buses too, and taxis are very cheap.
 What is the topic: tourist attractions or transportation?*

. . . .

5 What is the topic: tourist attractions or hotels?
 – You should go to the museum. It's very famous. And there are lots of temples and traditional buildings, like the hotel in the old part of the city. The best way to see everything is on foot.
 What is the topic: tourist attractions or hotels?*

. . . .

6 What is the topic: shopping or industry?
 – You can get very nice clothes there at reasonable prices. Electronic items like cameras and radios are also very good bargains.
 What is the topic: shopping or industry?*

. . . .

Unit 4   What a story!

Unit 4, Exercise 1

Listen to a statement about an event, followed by a Wh-word, like this:
– There was a bank robbery downtown this morning.
– Where.

Ask a question with the Wh-word, like this:
– *Where* **was the bank robbery?**

Then you will hear a reply. Listen to another example.
– There was a traffic accident on the freeway last night.
– When.*
– *When* **was the traffic accident?**
– Last night, around 10.

Ready.

1 There was a fire in the Carlyle Hotel on Sunday.
  Where.*
  . . . .
  In the Carlyle Hotel.
2 There was an earthquake in South America yesterday.
  When.*
  . . . .
  Yesterday morning.
3 A plane crashed yesterday because of engine trouble.
  Why.*
  . . . .
  Because of engine trouble.
4 There was a bank robbery on Main Street this morning.
  Where.*
  . . . .
  On Main Street.
5 The robber got away in a stolen car.
  How.*
  . . . .
  By stealing a car.

Unit 4, Exercise 2

Listen to people talking about news events. What topic are they talking about? Listen to an example, like this:
– What is the topic: an art exhibition or a concert?

– It was very crowded. There were lots of interesting paintings on display. And some of the artists were there to answer questions about their paintings.
– What is the topic: an art exhibition or a concert?*
– **An art exhibition.**

Ready.

1 What is the topic: a traffic accident or an earthquake?
  – It sure was scary! Lots of buildings were damaged and several bridges collapsed. But luckily no one was killed.
  What is the topic: traffic accident or an earthquake?*
  . . . .
2 What is the topic: a fire or a robbery?
  – It started about midnight. Most of the hotel guests were asleep. As soon as the alarm went off everybody got out of the building as quickly as they could. Luckily only one floor of the hotel was damaged, and no one was hurt.
  What is the topic: a fire or a robbery?*
  . . . .
3 What is the topic: a sports event or a concert?
  – There must have been about 20,000 people there – it was a huge crowd. Unfortunately the visiting team played really well that day. They won 25 to nothing.
  What is the topic: a sports event or a concert?*
  . . . .
4 What is the topic: a robbery or a lottery?
  – I was really surprised when I learned I had won $25,000. I don't know what I'll do with the money. Maybe I'll take a trip around the world.
  What is the topic: a robbery or a lottery?*
  . . . .
5 What is the topic: a storm or a drought?
  – It was one of the worst ones we had this year. The wind was very strong and it rained for three days. Lots of trees were blown over, and many houses were damaged.
  What is the topic: a storm or a drought?*
  . . . .

(Unit 4 continues on next page.)

Unit 4, Exercise 3

Reply to each question about a news event like this:
– Did you hear about the fire downtown?*
– No, I didn't know there was a fire downtown.

Ready.

1 Did you hear about the fire downtown?*
. . . .

2 Did you hear about the earthquake in California?*
. . . .

3 Did you hear about the party at City Hall last night?*
. . . .

4 Did you hear about the accident on the freeway?*
. . . .

5 Did you hear about the fight at the rock concert?*
. . . .

Unit 4, Exercise 4

Listen to people describe things that happened to them. Respond like this:
– Someone ran into my car!*
– Someone ran into your car? When did that happen?

Then you will hear a reply, like this:
– This morning.

Respond like this:
– That's too bad.

Listen to another example.
– I got fired from my job.*
– You got fired from your job? When did that happen?
– Yesterday.*
– That's too bad.

Ready.

1 I lost my wallet.*
. . . .
This morning.*
. . . .

2 Someone broke into my apartment.*
. . . .
Over the weekend.*
. . . .

3 I lost my keys.*
. . . .
On Tuesday, I think.*
. . . .

4 I got stopped for speeding.*
. . . .
This morning.*
. . . .

5 I had a car accident.*
. . . .
On Sunday.*
. . . .

Unit 4, Exercise 5

[*Note:* This conversation is on page 25 of the Student's Book.]

Listen to this conversation.

A: You know, I had a really strange dream last night.
B: Oh yeah? What was it about?
A: Well, I dreamed that I was driving in the country late at night when I saw a UFO land on the road in front of me.
B: And then what happened?
A: Well, first, I got out of my car. While I was standing there, this strange green creature came out of the UFO. I tried to run away, but I couldn't move. Then, as it was coming nearer, it put out its hand and touched my face. It felt wet and horrible!
B: Ugh! And . . . ?
A: And then I woke up and found my cat on my pillow. It was licking my face!

Now repeat each sentence. Ready.

Unit 4, Exercise 6

Answer these questions about a traffic accident with the second choice, like this:
– Was your friend driving or were you driving the car?*
– **I was driving the car.**

Ready.

1 Was your friend driving or were you driving the car?*
. . . .
2 Was it a clear night or was it raining?*
. . . .
3 Were you talking to your friend or were you paying attention to the road?*
. . . .
4 Was the car in front of you making a right turn or a left turn?*
. . . .
5 Were you speeding up or slowing down?*
. . . .
6 Were you driving without a seat belt or were you wearing a seat belt?*
. . . .

Unit 4, Exercise 7

Listen to a statement, like this:
– Something interesting happened while I was driving to work today.

Ask what happened, like this:
– **Really? What happened while you were driving to work?**

Then you will hear a response. Listen to another example.
– Something interesting happened while I was shopping.*
– **Really? What happened while you were shopping?**
– I saw someone shoplifting.

Ready.

1 Something exciting happened when I was walking downtown.*
. . . .
I saw a movie star.
2 Something interesting happened while I was waiting at the airport.*
. . . .
I saw the President.
3 Something interesting happened when I was coming home on the bus.*
. . . .
The bus broke down and we had to walk a mile for help.
4 Something interesting happened while I was swimming this morning.*
. . . .
I found a diamond ring at the bottom of the pool.
5 Something embarrassing happened while I was taking a shower.*
. . . .
My dinner guests arrived!

Unit 5 Could you do me a favor?

Unit 5, Exercise 1

Make a request using "Could you" and "Please,"
like this:
– Open the window.*
– **Could you open the window, please?**

Then you will hear a reply. Listen to another
example.
– Pass me that book.*
– **Could you pass me that book, please?**
– Yes, here you are.

Ready.

1 Take these books to the library.*

. . . .
Sure. I'll do it this afternoon.
2 Help me with this exercise.*

. . . .
Sure. What's the problem?
3 Give me a ride home after class.*

. . . .
I'm sorry, but I didn't drive my car today.
4 Change a one-hundred dollar bill for me.*

. . . .
Sorry, I don't have change for a hundred
dollars.
5 Lend me your car on Saturday.*

. . . .
No way. The last time you borrowed my car
you had an accident!
6 Mail these letters for me.*

. . . .
OK. I'll mail them after class.
7 Let me use your dictionary.*

. . . .
Yeah. Help yourself.

Unit 5, Exercise 2

Make a request using "Would you mind," like
this:
– Close the window.*
– **Would you mind closing the window?**

Then listen to the reply. Listen to another
example.
– Type this letter for me.*
– **Would you mind typing this letter for
me?**
– Sorry, I can't type.

Ready.

1 Lend me fifty dollars.*

. . . .
No, you still owe me twenty-five dollars
from last week!

2 Drive me to the airport.*

. . . .
OK. What time do you need to leave?
3 Lend me your class notes.*

. . . .
No problem. Here you are.
4 Help me prepare this report.*

. . . .
OK. As soon as I finish typing this letter.
5 Let me use your phone.*

. . . .
OK. It's in the hallway.

Unit 5, Exercise 3

Listen to people making requests. Did the
second speaker agree or refuse? Listen to this
example.
A: I wonder if I could borrow your car on
Sunday.
B: Well, actually, I have to take my sister to
the airport. Sorry.
– Did the second speaker agree or refuse?*
– **Refuse.**

Ready.

1 A: Could you lend me this magazine for the
weekend?
  B: No problem. I'm finished with it. It has
some really interesting articles.
  Did the second speaker agree or refuse?*

. . . .
2 A: I wonder if you'd be able to help me move
into my new apartment on Saturday.
  B: Well, I'm not doing much this weekend.
What time do you want me to come over?
  Did the second speaker agree or refuse?*

. . . .
3 A: I wonder if you'd be able to help me with
my class project on Thursday night.
  B: Gee, I wish I could, but Thursday night is
when I have my karate class.
  Did the second speaker agree or refuse?*

. . . .
4 A: Would you mind turning off the TV?
  B: Well, I'm waiting for the news. I want to
find out what's happening in the elections.
  Did the second speaker agree or refuse?*

. . . .
5 A: Would you be able to read my essay for
me and see if I made any mistakes?
  B: Well, I'd really love to read your essay,
but I haven't finished my homework yet.
Why don't you ask Maria?
  Did the second speaker agree or refuse?*

. . . .

Unit 5, Exercise 4

Listen to people ask you to do something.
Politely refuse, like this:
- I wonder if you'd mind taking me to the airport tonight.*
- **Oh, I'm sorry. I can't take you to the airport tonight.**

Ready.

1 I wonder if you'd mind taking me to the airport tonight.*
....
2 I wonder if you'd mind typing these letters.*
....
3 I wonder if you'd mind taking these books back to the library.*
....
4 I wonder if you'd mind checking my homework.*
....
5 I wonder if you'd mind lending me your car.*
....
6 I wonder if you'd mind lending me fifty dollars.*
....
7 I wonder if you'd mind helping me with my homework.*
....

Unit 5, Exercise 5

[*Note:* This conversation is on page 31 of the Student's Book.]

Listen to this conversation.

A: Hello?
B: Hello. Can I speak to Sophia, please?
A: I'm sorry, she's not in right now. Would you like to leave a message?
B: Yes, please. This is Harry. Would you tell her that Tony's having a party on Saturday?
A: Sure.
B: And please ask her if she'd like to go with me.
A: All right, Peter. I'll give her the message.
B: No, this is Harry, not Peter!
A: Oh, sorry.
B: By the way, who's Peter?

Now repeat each sentence. Ready.

Unit 5, Exercise 6

Ask someone to give messages to Sue, like this:
- Jack's having a party tonight.*
- **Could you tell Sue that Jack's having a party tonight?**

Listen to another example.
- There's a tennis game on Saturday.*
- **Could you tell Sue that there's a tennis game on Saturday?**

Ready.

1 The meeting tomorrow has been canceled.*
....
2 There's a letter for her in the office.*
....
3 Don't be late for our appointment.*
....
4 I'll call her at 9 p.m. tomorrow.*
....
5 There's an interesting movie playing downtown.*
....
6 Don't forget to return the money she borrowed.*
....

Unit 6 Comparatively speaking

Unit 6, Exercise 1

Answer the questions with the second choice, like this:
- Would you rather learn the piano or the guitar?*
- **I'd rather learn the guitar.**
- Would you rather live in a house or an apartment?*
- **I'd rather live in an apartment.**

Ready.

1 Would you rather live in the city or in the suburbs?*
. . . .
2 Would you rather study at a large or a small university?*
. . . .
3 Would you rather have a motorcycle or a car?*
. . . .
4 Would you rather travel by air or by train?*
. . . .
5 Would you rather send your children to a public school or a private school?*
. . . .
6 Would you rather live in a house or an apartment?*
. . . .

Unit 6, Exercise 2

Ask a question with "Would rather," like this:
- work outdoors or indoors*
- **Would you rather work outdoors or indoors?**

Then you will hear a reply. Listen to another example.
- listen to classical music or pop music*
- **Would you rather listen to classical music or pop music?**
- Oh, I prefer classical music.

Ready.

1 work outdoors or indoors*
. . . .
I'd rather work outdoors.
2 see a movie in a theater or rent a video*
. . . .
Mmm . . . I'd rather rent a video.

3 study English in Australia or Canada*
. . . .
Australia, I think, because it's warmer there.
4 learn the guitar or the piano*
. . . .
I'd rather learn the piano.
5 be a teacher or an actor*
. . . .
I'd rather be a teacher, I think.
6 work for someone else or be self-employed*
. . . .
That's easy! I'd rather be self-employed.

Unit 6, Exercise 3

Answer each question with the second choice. Then ask a follow-up question, like this:
- Do you prefer studying part-time or full-time?*
- **I prefer studying full-time. How about you?**

Then you will hear a response. Listen to another example.
- Do you prefer reading or watching TV?*
- **I prefer watching TV. How about you?**
- Oh, I prefer reading.

Ready.

1 Do you prefer studying part-time or full-time?*
. . . .
So do I.
2 Do you prefer studying in a large class or a small class?*
. . . .
So do I.
3 Do you prefer playing tennis or golf?*
. . . .
I do too.
4 Do you prefer swimming at the beach or in a pool?*
. . . .
Well, I prefer the beach.
5 Do you prefer reading novels or magazines?*
. . . .
I like them both.
6 Do you prefer traveling by ship or by air?*
. . . .
Not me. I prefer traveling by ship.

Unit 6, Exercise 4

[*Note:* This conversation is on page 34 of the Student's Book.]

Listen to this conversation.

ANN: Would you rather send your children to a public or a private school?
TOM: Mmm, I'd rather send them to a public school, I think.
ANN: Oh, why?
TOM: Well, it's cheaper for one thing . . .
ANN: Yes, but do you think the teachers are as good in the public schools?
TOM: Oh, yeah, I went to a public high school, and I had very good teachers there.

Now repeat each sentence. Ready.

Unit 6, Exercise 5

Answer the questions with the first choice.
Then ask a follow-up question, like this:
– Is your sister teaching at an elementary school or a secondary school?*
– **She's teaching at an elementary school. Where is your sister teaching?**

Then you will hear a response. Listen to another example.
– Do you go to a public school or a private school?*
– **I go to a public school. Where do you go?**
– I go to a public school too.

Ready.

1 Are you studying at a technical college or a university?*

. . . .
I'm not studying anymore. I graduated last month.
2 Does your brother teach at a community college or a high school?*

. . . .
He teaches at a high school.
3 Are you studying literature or philosophy?*

. . . .
I'm studying physics.
4 Do you have classes in the daytime or in the evening?*

. . . .
I have both daytime *and* evening classes.
5 Do you teach at a high school or a technical school?*

. . . .
I teach first grade at an elementary school.

Unit 6, Exercise 6

Answer the questions like this:
– Do a lot of students go to school until they're 16 here?*
– **Yes, in fact most students go to school until they're 16 here.**

– Do a lot of colleges teach French?*
– **Yes, in fact most colleges teach French.**

Ready.

1 Do a lot of students go to school until they're 16 here?*

. . . .
2 Do a lot of colleges teach French?*

. . . .
3 Do a lot of students take English in high school?*

. . . .
4 Do a lot of teachers have a college degree?*

. . . .
5 Do a lot of colleges have dorms?*

. . . .
6 Do a lot of students finish high school?*

. . . .

(Unit 6 continues on next page.)

Unit 6, Exercise 7

Listen to statements about education. Ask for clarification by repeating each statement, like this:
– Very few schools teach Korean.*
– **Did you say that very few schools teach Korean?**

Then you will hear a reply. Listen to another example.
– Neither teachers nor students wear uniforms.*
– **Did you say that neither teachers nor students wear uniforms?**
– That's right.

Ready.

1 Not many schools have language labs.*

....
    Yes, that's right.

2 Not all primary schools teach English.*

....
    Yes, I did.

3 A few schools have Saturday classes.*

....
    Yes, that's what I said.

4 Both elementary schools and high schools have large classes.*

....
    Yes, they both have large classes.

5 None of the private schools is cheap.*

....
    Yes, in fact they're quite expensive.

6 Most high schools don't have school uniforms.*

....
    Yes, although some private high schools do.

Unit 7 Don't drink the water

Unit 7, Exercise 1

Practice saying consonant clusters with /s/.
Listen and repeat. Ready.

1 The cost of the trip includes plane tickets
   and bus trips.*
2 The flight to the east coast lasts for three
   hours and fifty minutes.*
3 The next flight leaves in just a few minutes.*
4 My father often makes trips to the bookshops
   to buy old books.*
5 There are lots of interesting ships down at
   the docks.*
6 A good journalist collects facts first and then
   writes.*

Unit 7, Exercise 2

Listen to a phrase, like this:
– to see old cities

Use it to complete this sentence:
– Many people visit Europe.

Listen to two examples:
– to see old cities*
– **Many people visit Europe to see old
  cities.**

– to shop*
– **Many people visit Europe to shop.**

Ready.

1 to enjoy the food*
. . . .
2 to see the museums and churches*
. . . .
3 to buy clothes*
. . . .
4 to see the old cities*
. . . .
5 to practice a foreign language.*
. . . .

Unit 7, Exercise 3

Report what each person says, like this:
WOMAN: I'm going to Spain. I want to learn
   Spanish.*
– **She's going to Spain so she can learn
  Spanish.**

MAN: I'm going to London. I want to find a job
   there.*
– **He's going to London so he can find a job
  there.**

Ready.

1 MAN: I'm going to Paris. I want to learn
   French.*
. . . .
2 WOMAN: I'm going to Los Angeles. I want to
   go to a friend's wedding.*
. . . .
3 MAN: I'm going to Switzerland. I want to do
   some skiing.*
. . . .
4 WOMAN: I'm going to Florida. I want to visit
   Disney World.*
. . . .
5 MAN: I'm going to Australia. I want to go
   camping.*
. . . .

Unit 7, Exercise 4

[*Note:* This conversation is on page 42 of the
Student's Book.]

Listen to this conversation.

A: I'm thinking of going to Brazil next year,
    Maria.
B: Oh, great! I'm sure you'll have a good time.
A: What places do tourists visit in Brazil?
B: Well, a lot of people go to Rio for Carnival.
    And nowadays, lots of people are visiting
    the Amazon to take river trips.
A: Oh, really? That sounds interesting. And
    when's a good time to visit?
B: Well, I like Rio in the spring or fall because
    it's not too hot then.

Now repeat each sentence. Ready.

(*Unit 7 continues on next page.*)

Unit 7, Exercise 5

Report each person's reasons with "because of," like this:

WOMAN: I don't like Hong Kong. There's too much pollution.*

– She doesn't like Hong Kong because of the pollution.

MAN: I like living in Italy. I really love the food.*

– He likes living in Italy because of the food.

Ready.

1 WOMAN: I like Brazil. The people are wonderful.*

. . . .

2 MAN: I enjoy living in Los Angeles. It has great nightlife.*

. . . .

3 WOMAN: I like traveling in Asia. The hotels are excellent.*

. . . .

4 WOMAN: I love Washington, D.C. It has fantastic museums.*

. . . .

5 MAN: I don't like Europe in the summer. There are too many tourists.*

. . . .

6 MAN: I love Italy. The food is great.*

. . . .

Unit 7, Exercise 6

Listen to people talk about different places. They say some good points and *one* problem. What problem do they mention? Listen to an example:

WOMAN: I loved my vacation in Thailand. The beaches were fantastic and the hotels were reasonably priced. Unfortunately it was very crowded because it was tourist season.

– What problem does she mention?*

– It was very crowded.

Listen to another example.

MAN: I enjoyed my trip a lot. The city had excellent museums, and I enjoyed the theater too. There was only one drawback: It wasn't safe at night. I had to be careful.

– What problem does he mention?*

– It wasn't safe at night.

Ready.

1 WOMAN: You have to visit Madrid. It's a wonderful city. I especially liked the nightlife – they have wonderful clubs and discos. I loved everything except the cars. Madrid has very heavy traffic. But the people are warm and friendly, and I can't wait to go back.

– What problem does she mention?*

. . . .

2 MAN: I went to a small town in the mountains for my vacation. It was very quiet and relaxing. No TV, no movies, just nature. That's the way I like it. But it's hard to enjoy yourself when there's terrible poverty all around you.

– What problem does he mention?*

. . . .

3 WOMAN: I stayed with friends last weekend. We had a good time, even though the buses and trains were on strike! We had to stay home because it was too hard to get anywhere in the city. So we just played some tennis, watched videos, and visited.

– What problem does she mention?*

. . . .

4 MAN: I just got back from Washington, D.C. You know, I went there to visit the museums and do some research for school. The museums were excellent, and the subway system was very clean and easy to use. My only disappointment was that the art gallery I wanted to visit was closed. They were doing some repairs.

– What problem does he mention?*

. . . .

5 WOMAN: My trip to Tokyo was incredible. The only bad thing I have to say is that my trip was too short! My hotel was excellent, the sightseeing was very interesting, and the people were really helpful and polite.

– What problem does she mention?*

. . . .

Unit 7, Exercise 7

You are talking to someone about customs in their country. Ask questions with "What happens when . . . " like this:

– You are invited to someone's house for dinner.*

– What happens when you are invited to someone's house for dinner?

Then you will hear a reply. Listen to another example.

– You meet someone for the first time.*

– What happens when you meet someone for the first time?

– Oh, you generally shake hands.

Ready.

1 You are invited to someone's house for dinner.*

. . . .
You usually bring a gift, like flowers or a bottle of wine.

2 You go out to dinner with friends.*

. . . .
You usually share the bill.

3 Your friend is going to have a baby.*

. . . .
Well, you have a party for her and give her gifts.

4 You make an appointment with someone.*

. . . .
You should arrive on time.

5 A friend has a birthday party.*

. . . .
You usually take a card, and perhaps a small gift.

6 You stay at someone's home.*

. . . .
It's nice to give them a gift, and also help out around the house.

Unit 8   Getting things done

Unit 8, Exercise 1

Ask where you can get things done, like this:
- a passport photo taken*
- **Do you know where I could get a passport photo taken?**

Then you will hear a reply. Listen to another example.
- my hair cut*
- **Do you know where I could get my hair cut?**
- Sure. There's a barber down the street, at the corner.

Ready.

1 a camera repaired*

. . . .

   Sure. You can get it repaired at the camera shop in the mall.
2 my shoes repaired*

. . . .

   No, I'm not really sure. Sorry.
3 color photocopies made*

. . . .

   I think there's a place on Fourth Street.
4 my stereo fixed*

. . . .

   Try the electronics store on Main Street.
5 a typewriter fixed*

. . . .

   No, I don't. Why don't you look in the phone book?
6 my car serviced*

. . . .

   Well, Danny's Auto Shop on Fourth Street is *my* favorite place.

Unit 8, Exercise 2

Listen to a guest at a hotel say things that need to be done, like this:
- I need to have these shoes repaired.

You are the hotel clerk. Reply like this:
- **Oh, I'll have them repaired for you.**

Listen to another example.
- I need to have this suit cleaned.*
- **Oh, I'll have it cleaned for you.**

Ready.

1 I need to have these shoes repaired.*

. . . .

2 I need to have this suit cleaned.*

. . . .

3 I need to have this film developed.*

. . . .

4 I need to have this fax sent.*

. . . .

5 I need to have this report typed.*

. . . .

Unit 8, Exercise 3

Practice the sounds /s/ and /sh/. Listen and repeat these sentences. Ready.
1 I'm looking for a store that sells washing machines.*
2 Should I have these silk shirts washed or dry cleaned?*
3 You can use this machine to get cash.*
4 It's not expensive to get your shoes shined on the street.*
5 I bought these sheets at a special sale on Saturday.*
6 My hair is a mess, so I'm getting it cut and shampooed.*

Unit 8, Exercise 4

[*Note:* This conversation is on page 51 of the Student's Book.]

Listen to this conversation.

A: I've got a friend coming for the weekend who loves jazz. Where's a good place to take her?
B: Uh, why not take her to the New Orleans Club? That's a great place to hear live music.
C: Yeah, but it's hard to get in on the weekend. I like the Back Door better because it's not so crowded.
A: Oh, yeah? Do they have dancing there?
C: Uh, I don't think so.

Now repeat each sentence. Ready.

Unit 8, Exercise 5

Listen to a phrase like this:
– hear live music

Ask a question using "Where's a good place to," like this:
– hear live music*
– Where's a good place to hear live music?

Listen to the reply, and then repeat the location and thank the speaker, like this:
– At the disco.*
– At the disco? OK, thanks.

Listen to the whole example again.
– hear live music*
– Where's a good place to hear live music?
– At the disco.*
– At the disco? OK, thanks.

Listen to another example.
– buy fresh seafood*
– Where's a good place to buy fresh seafood?
– At the fish market downtown.*
– At the fish market downtown? OK, thanks.

Ready.

1 buy CDs*

. . . .
There's a good music store at the mall.*

. . . .

2 have Italian food*

. . . .
There's a great Italian restaurant in the Park Hotel.*

. . . .

3 buy books*

. . . .
There's a good bookstore near the university.*

. . . .

4 try local food*

. . . .
Try the restaurants in the Old Town.*

. . . .

5 buy interesting souvenirs*

. . . .
Try the market near the train station.*

. . . .

6 see interesting architecture*

. . . .
The best place is around City Hall.*

. . . .

(Unit 8 continues on next page.)

Unit 8, Exercise 6

Listen to a question. Then you will hear
someone describing a place. Answer the
question, like this:
– What is she describing: a disco, a library, or a
bank?
FEMALE: It's always busy. A lot of tourists go
   there to change traveler's checks. And of
   course it's in the business district, so a lot of
   businesses have accounts there. But the
   service is quick and efficient, and the tellers
   are very friendly.
– What is she describing: a disco, a library, or a
bank?*
– A bank.

Ready.

1 What is she describing: a bank, a restaurant,
   or a market?
   FEMALE: I like it there. Everything is really
      cheap, and the quality is pretty good too.
      Plus it's lively, so it's a fun place to shop.
   – What is she describing: a bank, a
      restaurant, or a market?*
   . . . .

2 What is he describing: a beach, an airport, or
   a building?
   MALE: It's one of my favorite places in the
      city. It's over 500 years old and was
      designed by a very famous architect. It's
      open to the public during the week but
      not on weekends.
   – What is he describing: a beach, an airport,
      or a building?*
   . . . .

3 What is she describing: a bookstore, a
   railway station, or a supermarket?
   WOMAN: It's probably the best of its kind in
      town. I like it because there is a large
      English section. And the salespeople are
      great. They let you spend as much time
      as you want reading. They don't pressure
      you to buy.
   – What is she describing: a bookstore, a
      railway station, or a supermarket?*
   . . . .

4 What is he describing: a supermarket, a
   music store, or a cafe?
   MALE: I often drop in there after class to get
      a bite to eat or to meet friends. They
      usually have live music there in the
      evenings.
   – What is he describing: a supermarket, a
      music store, or a cafe?*
   . . . .

5 What is she describing: a restaurant, a park,
   or a store?
   FEMALE: It's a nice place to go and relax. It's
      quiet and very pretty in the summer,
      when all the flowers are out. Lots of
      people go there to eat their lunch when
      the weather is nice.
   – What is she describing: a restaurant, a
      park, or a store?*
   . . . .

Unit 8, Exercise 7

Answer questions about different places, like
this:
– Is the nightclub noisy?*
– No, I like it because it's not so noisy.

– Is the beach crowded?*
– No, I like it because it's not so crowded.

Ready.

1 Is the park usually crowded?*
   . . . .
2 Is the jazz club expensive?*
   . . . .
3 Is the New Orleans Club very noisy?*
   . . . .
4 Is the swimming pool very deep?*
   . . . .
5 Is the bookstore usually busy?*
   . . . .

Unit 9   Is that a fact?

Unit 9, Exercise 1

You will hear four numbers. What year do they describe? Listen and say the year, like this:
- 1, 9, 2, 3*
- **The year nineteen twenty-three.**

- 1, 5, 0, 0*
- **The year fifteen hundred.**

Ready.

1 1, 9, 2, 3*
. . . .
2 1, 5, 0 , 0*
. . . .
3 1, 8, 9, 6*
. . . .
4 1, 9, 6, 9*
. . . .
5 1, 7, 0, 5*
. . . .
6 2, 0, 0, 1*
. . . .

Unit 9, Exercise 2

You will hear an event like this:
- the first flight in a jumbo jet

Ask a question with "When was . . . ," like this:
- **When was the first flight in a jumbo jet?**

Then you will hear a reply. Listen to another example.
- the first satellite launched*
- **When was the first satellite launched?**
- In the late fifties, I believe.

Ready.

1 the first flight in a jumbo jet*
. . . .
In 1970.
2 the first subway opened*
. . . .
In 1863.
3 the first compact disc sold*
. . . .
In 1983.
4 the first color movie shown*
. . . .
I think it was in 1930.
5 plastic invented*
. . . .
In 1909.
6 the first personal computer sold*
. . . .
In 1975.

Unit 9, Exercise 3

Listen to a statement about a past event, like this:
- World War One began.

Ask a question with "When did," like this:
- **When did World War One begin?**

Then you will hear the answer. Listen to another example.
- World War Two ended.*
- **When did World War Two end?**
- In 1945.

Ready.

1 World War One began.*
. . . .
In 1914.
2 The first person traveled in space.*
. . . .
In 1961.
3 Jazz first became popular.*
. . . .
In the 1920s.
4 George Orwell published the novel *1984*.*
. . . .
In 1949.
5 The French Revolution began.*
. . . .
In 1789.
6 Japan began trading with China.*
. . . .
In the year 606.

Unit 9, Exercise 4

[*Note:* This conversation is on page 57 of the Student's Book.]

Listen to this conversation.

A: I've just been reading an interesting article about robots. Did you know that the typical factory worker in the future will be a robot?
B: Really? That's scary.
A: Yeah, and they'll even use robots to make and repair other robots.
B: That's hard to imagine. And when is this supposed to happen?
A: Within thirty years. And robots will also be building factories in outer space and even mining minerals on the moon.
B: Hey, maybe by then they'll have invented a robot to clean my apartment!

Now listen and repeat each sentence. Ready.

Unit 9, Exercise 5

Listen to a phrase. Then ask questions about
what will happen in five years, like this:
– living in the same place*
– **Do you think you'll be living in the same
place in five years?**

Then you will hear a reply. Listen to another
example.
– have the same friends*
– **Do you think you'll have the same
friends in five years?**
– No, I'll probably have lots of new friends in
five years.

Ready.

1 be living in the same place*
. . . .
I hope not.
2 have the same job*
. . . .
Yes, probably. I like my job.
3 be driving the same car*
. . . .
Probably not. My car is already 15 years old!
4 look any different*
. . . .
I'd rather not think about it.
5 dress any differently*
. . . .
I'm not sure.
6 own your own home*
. . . .
I hope so.

Unit 9, Exercise 6

Listen to predictions about the year 2050.
Disagree by making a negative statement, like
this:
– People will be living on the moon.*
– **Oh, I don't think people will be living on
the moon.**

– They will have discovered a cure for cancer.*
– **Oh, I don't think they will have
discovered a cure for cancer.**

Ready.

1 People will be living on the moon.*
. . . .
2 They will have discovered a cure for cancer.*
. . . .
3 They will have discovered a way to prevent
aging.*
. . . .
4 People will be driving electric cars.*
. . . .
5 Cities will be built under the ocean.*
. . . .
6 They will have found a cure for baldness.*
. . . .
7 Everyone will be speaking English.*
. . . .

Unit 10 There's no place like home

Unit 10, Exercise 1

Reply to questions about household chores, like this:
– Do you like washing dishes?*
– **No, I can't stand washing dishes. How about you?**

Then you will hear a reply. Listen to another example.
– Do you like vacuuming?*
– **No, I can't stand vacuuming. How about you?**
– I can't stand it either.

Ready.

1 Do you like cleaning bathrooms?*
. . . .
I can't stand it either.
2 Do you like scrubbing floors?*
. . . .
Oh, I don't mind it once in a while.
3 Do you like ironing clothes?*
. . . .
Oh, it's OK, I guess.
4 Do you like doing laundry?*
. . . .
I'm not crazy about it either.
5 Do you like washing dishes?*
. . . .
Oh, I enjoy it.
6 Do you like cleaning the yard?*
. . . .
I like it. I enjoy being outside.

Unit 10, Exercise 2

Answer questions about a house or an apartment, like this:
– Does it have a kitchen and a laundry room?*
– **It has a kitchen, but it doesn't have a laundry room.**

– Does it have a patio and a yard?*
– **It has a patio, but it doesn't have a yard.**

Ready.

1 Does it have a living room and a dining room?*
. . . .
2 Does it have a garden and a pool?*
. . . .
3 Does it have a yard and a patio?*
. . . .

4 Does it have central heating and air conditioning?*
. . . .
5 Does it have a balcony and a view?*
. . . .
6 Does it have a bathtub and a shower?*
. . . .

Unit 10, Exercise 3

Answer the questions you hear about a town or neighborhood, like this:
– Is there a good bus system and a subway?*
– **Yes, there's a good bus system as well as a subway.**

– Is there a shopping mall and a market?*
– **Yes, there's a shopping mall as well as a market.**

Ready.

1 Is there an elementary school and a high school?*
. . . .
2 Is there a park and a public swimming pool?*
. . . .
3 Is there a gas station and a supermarket?*
. . . .
4 Is there a taxi stand and a bus stop?*
. . . .
5 Is there a bank and a post office?*
. . . .
6 Is there a shopping mall and a department store?*
. . . .

Unit 10, Exercise 4

[*Note:* This conversation is on page 62 of the Student's Book.]

Listen to this conversation.

A: Have you moved to your new apartment yet, Fred?
B: Yes, we moved in last Saturday.
A: So, how do you like it?
B: Oh, it's great! There's plenty of room, and it's quiet too.
A: Yeah? Uh, what's the building like? Does it have a pool?
B: No, it doesn't have a pool, but there's a patio downstairs and a big yard for the kids to play in.
A: It sounds nice.
B: It is. Why don't you come over this weekend and see it?
A: OK. I'd like to.

Now repeat each sentence. Ready.

Unit 10, Exercise 5

Answer questions about a neighborhood, like this:
- Is there a shopping mall and a department store?*
- **There's no shopping mall, although there's a department store.**

- Is there a movie theater and a good video store?*
- **There's no movie theater, although there's a good video store.**

Ready.

1 Is there a subway and a good bus system?*
. . . .

2 Is there a park and a public swimming pool?*
. . . .

3 Is there a shopping center and a market?*
. . . .

4 Is there a restaurant and a fast food store?*
. . . .

5 Is there a post office and a bank?*
. . . .

6 Is there a bookstore and a library?*
. . . .

Unit 10, Exercise 6

Listen to people talking to their apartment manager about problems in their apartment. Reply with the second choice, like this:
- What's the problem? Is it the bedroom fan or the kitchen fan?*
- **It's the *kitchen* fan.**

Pay attention to stress. Listen to another example.
- What's the problem? Is it the bathroom window or the bedroom window?*
- **It's the *bedroom* window.**

Ready.

1 What's the problem? Is it the bedroom fan or the kitchen fan?*
. . . .

2 Which one is stuck? Is it the bathroom window or the bedroom window?*
. . . .

3 What's wrong? Is it the kitchen light or the bathroom light?*
. . . .

4 Where's the leak? Is it the hot water faucet or the cold water faucet?*
. . . .

5 Which one is broken? Is it the living room air conditioner or the bedroom air conditioner?*
. . . .

6 Which door needs repairing? Is it the front door or the back door?*
. . . .

7 Which telephone doesn't work? Is it the one in the bedroom or the one in the kitchen?*
. . . .

Unit 10, Exercise 7

Listen to people talking about a problem with something in their apartment. Listen and say what they are talking about, like this.

– Is she talking about the TV, the lamp, or the iron?

WOMAN: I noticed that the room was getting darker. Then it started to make a strange buzzing sound. So I unplugged it and called a repairperson immediately.

– Is she talking about the TV, the lamp, or the iron?*

– The lamp.

Ready.

1 Is she talking about the stove, the refrigerator, or the air conditioner?

WOMAN: Something's definitely wrong. It's not cooling properly. The food that I put in it yesterday was spoiled by today.

– Is she talking about the stove, the refrigerator, or the air conditioner?*

. . . .

2 Is he talking about the radio, the television, or the telephone?

MAN: It's been out of order for several hours. I can't get a dial tone. I'd like to get it fixed as soon as possible because I have to make some important business calls.

– Is he talking about the radio, the television, or the telephone?*

. . . .

3 Is he talking about the bedroom, the living room, or the kitchen?

MAN: I wish you could fix the central heating in there. When I go to bed at night it's so cold that I can't get to sleep.

– Is he talking about the bedroom, the living room, or the kitchen?*

. . . .

4 Is she talking about the stove, the dryer, or the central heating?

WOMAN: It hasn't been heating right for some time. Sometimes it gets too hot and burns everything. Other times it doesn't get hot enough, and things don't get cooked.

– Is she talking about the stove, the dryer, or the central heating?*

. . . .

5 Is he talking about the central heating, the lamp, or the air conditioner?

MAN: It's been driving me crazy all summer! It keeps breaking down and it doesn't keep the room cool. It's so hot in this room most of the time that I can hardly breathe.

– Is he talking about the central heating, the lamp, or the air conditioner?*

. . . .

Unit 11   What a world we live in!

Unit 11, Exercise 1

[*Note:* This conversation is on page 68 of the Student's Book.]

Listen to this conversation.

A: Did you hear that Jerry lost his job?
B: Oh, he did? Gee, that's too bad.
A: Yeah, the company wasn't making money, so they had to lay off some employees.
B: So what's Jerry going to do now?
A: Well, he's thinking of starting his own business.
B: Oh, that's great. I don't know what I'd do if I lost my job. Maybe I'd go back to school. What would you do?
A: Well, first I think I'd probably take a vacation. After that, I guess I'd try working for myself too.

Now repeat each sentence. Ready.

Unit 11, Exercise 2

You will hear a situation. Ask a question using "What would you do?" like this:
– Suppose you lost your job.*
– **What would you do if you lost your job?**

Then you will hear a reply. Listen to another example.
– Suppose you became president of your country.*
– **What would you do if you became president of your country?**
– I'd give everyone a job.

Ready.

1 Suppose you lost your job.*
. . . .
I'd look for another one.
2 Suppose you won the lottery.*
. . . .
I'd start my own business.
3 Suppose someone asked you for a big loan.*
. . . .
I'd tell them to go to a bank.
4 Suppose you found a lot of money on the street.*
. . . .
I'd take it to the police.
5 Suppose you could start your own business.*
. . . .
I'd open a restaurant.

6 Suppose you could live in a foreign country.*
. . . .
I'd move to Alaska.

Unit 11, Exercise 3

Listen to people saying what they would do if they won a million dollars. Report what they say like this:
WOMAN: What would I do? Buy a boat and sail around the world.*
– **She'd buy a boat and sail around the world.**

MAN: What would I do? Marry my childhood sweetheart.*
– **He'd marry his childhood sweetheart.**

Ready.

1 WOMAN: What would I do? Buy a boat and sail around the world.*
. . . .
2 MAN: What would I do? Move to California and become an artist.*
. . . .
3 MAN: What would I do? Give it all away.*
. . . .
4 WOMAN: What would I do? Stop working and go back to school.*
. . . .
5 MAN: What would I do? Buy myself a house and a car.*
. . . .
6 WOMAN: What would I do? Go into politics and run for mayor.*
. . . .

Unit 11, Exercise 4

Practice these sentences with plural "s." Listen and repeat. Ready.

1 Families in apartments shouldn't keep pets.*
2 Drivers who have large cars should pay higher taxes.*
3 Workers in government offices receive good benefits.*
4 It often takes weeks to answer letters from friends and relatives.*
5 Students with overdue library books must pay a fine of ten dollars.*

Unit 11, Exercise 5

Listen to two people talking, like this:
A: What if the government raised taxes?
B: People would complain.

Report what they say, like this:
– If the government raised taxes, people would complain.

Listen to another example.
A: What if employers raised salaries?
B: People would spend more.*
– If employers raised salaries, people would spend more.

Ready.

1 A: What if the government raised taxes?
  B: People would complain.*
  . . . .

2 A: What if people had smaller families?
  B: We might need fewer schools.*
  . . . .

3 A: What if cars were banned in cities?
  B: There would be less pollution.*
  . . . .

4 A: What if everyone spoke English well?
  B: There would be no jobs for English teachers.*
  . . . .

5 A: What if banks charged lower interest rates?
  B: More people could buy homes.*
  . . . .

Unit 11, Exercise 6

Someone is talking to you about problems in a country you have visited recently. Answer the questions like this:
– Is reducing the air pollution a problem there?*
– Yes, reducing air pollution is a real problem.

– Is controlling drugs a problem there?*
– Yes, controlling drugs is a real problem.

Ready.

1 Is reducing air pollution a problem there?*
  . . . .

2 Is keeping drugs off the streets a problem there?*
  . . . .

3 Is finding cheap housing a problem there?*
  . . . .

4 Is controlling traffic noise a problem there?*
  . . . .

5 Is finding jobs for graduates a problem there?*
  . . . .

6 Is making the cities safer a problem there?*
  . . . .

7 Is reducing unemployment a problem there?*
  . . . .

(Unit 11 continues on next page.)

Unit 11, Exercise 7

Listen to people giving opinions. What topics are they talking about? Listen to an example.
– What is she talking about: pollution, inflation, or traffic?

WOMAN: I wish we had a subway system in this city. I can't stand driving to work anymore. You know, it's only a 15-minute drive, but during rush hour it takes me an *hour*.

– What is she talking about: pollution, inflation, or traffic?*

– Traffic.

Ready.

1 What is he talking about: pollution, inflation, or traffic?

MAN: It's really time the government did something about it. It's not only the air we breathe that's so bad. It's also the beaches. The water isn't clean enough to swim in anymore. It's a shame.

– What is he talking about: pollution, inflation, or traffic?*

. . . .

2 What is she talking about: employment, crime, or public housing?

WOMAN: I don't go out alone at night anymore. I don't think it's safe. And I never leave my car parked downtown. Otherwise it's likely to get stolen.

– What is she talking about: employment, crime, or public housing?*

. . . .

3 What is he talking about: noise, poverty, or traffic?

MAN: It's OK if you leave before 6 o'clock in the morning to drive to work. But if you leave any later than that it's impossible to get to work on time. I hate to say it, but we need to build more freeways. It's getting more and more difficult to drive from one side of the city to the other during rush hours.

– What is he talking about: noise, poverty, or traffic?*

. . . .

4 What is she talking about: education, unemployment, or inflation?

WOMAN: The situation seems to be getting worse. More and more students find there is no job waiting for them when they graduate. And more and more people are losing their jobs too.

– What is she talking about: education, unemployment, or inflation?*

. . . .

5 What is she talking about: crime, drugs, or smoking?

WOMAN: These days it's banned almost everywhere: in most public places, in the workplace, even on airplanes. It's just not fair. A little smoke never hurt anyone.

– What is she talking about: crime, drugs, or smoking?*

. . . .

Unit 12   How does it work?

Unit 12, Exercise 1

[*Note:* This conversation is on page 74 of the Student's Book.]

Listen to this conversation.

A: Are you good at crossword puzzles?
B: Well, sometimes.
A: OK. What's this? It's a small piece of curved wire that's used for holding sheets of paper together.
B: Gee, I have no idea.
A: All right. Then how about this one? This instrument, which is usually made of metal or plastic, is used for eating food. It has a handle at one end and two or more points at the other.
B: I'm sorry. I can't guess that one either.

Now listen and repeat each sentence. Ready.

Unit 12, Exercise 2

Make a sentence using "that," like this:
– a machine for cleaning floors*
– **It's a machine that's used for cleaning floors.**

– a liquid for cleaning glass*
– **It's a liquid that's used for cleaning glass.**

Ready.

1 a tool for cutting wire*
. . . .
2 a container for holding liquids*
. . . .
3 a utensil for cutting paper*
. . . .
4 a gadget for opening bottles*
. . . .
5 a machine for cleaning carpets*
. . . .
6 a tool for chopping wood*
. . . .

Unit 12, Exercise 3

Ask a question with "What's the stuff that's used" and the phrase you hear, like this:
– to stick things together*
– **What's the stuff that's used to stick things together?**

Then you will hear a reply. Listen to another example.
– to polish floors*

– What's the stuff that's used to polish floors?
– Oh, that's called wax.

Ready.

1 to clean shoes*
. . . .
Oh, that's shoe polish.
2 to clean your teeth*
. . . .
It's called toothpaste.
3 used to make plants grow*
. . . .
It's called fertilizer.
4 used to wash clothes*
. . . .
Oh, that's detergent.
5 to stick things together*
. . . .
It's called glue.
6 to clean wood*
. . . .
It's called polish.

Unit 12, Exercise 4

Answer the questions you hear with the second choice, like this:
– Are you looking for the cassette player or the tape recorder?*
– **The *tape* recorder.**

Pay attention to stress. Listen to another example.
– Are you looking for the coffee machine or the rice cooker?*
– **The *rice* cooker.**

Ready.

1 Are you looking for the paper clips or the letter opener?*
. . . .
2 Are you looking for the bookshelf or the coffee table?*
. . . .
3 Are you looking for the swimming pool or the tennis court?*
. . . .
4 Are you looking for the pencil sharpener or the paper clips?*
. . . .
5 Are you looking for the letter opener or the pocket knife?*
. . . .
6 Are you looking for the floor polish or the soap powder?*
. . . .

Unit 12, Exercise 5

Answer each question with the first choice, like this:
- Are tires usually made of rubber or plastic?*
- **They're usually made of rubber.**

- Are windows usually made of glass or plastic?*
- **They're usually made of glass.**

Ready.

1 Are soft contact lenses usually made of plastic or glass?*
. . . .
2 Are shoes usually made of leather or rubber?*
. . . .
3 Are coins usually made of metal or plastic?*
. . . .
4 Are bottles usually made of glass or steel?*
. . . .
5 Are carpets usually made of wool or cotton?*
. . . .

Unit 12, Exercise 6

Listen to people asking about things that need to be done and reply like this:
- Do you want me to clean the living room?*
- **Yes, it needs to be cleaned.**

- Do you want me to wash the dishes?*
- **Yes, they need to be washed.**

Ready.

1 Do you want me to clean the living room?*
. . . .
2 Do you want me to wash the dishes?*
. . . .
3 Do you want me to water the plants?*
. . . .
4 Do you want me to take out the garbage?*
. . . .
5 Do you want me to iron the clothes?*
. . . .

Unit 12, Exercise 7

Listen to someone asking for information. Reply like this.
- Do you grow these plants inside?*
- **Yes, they're grown inside.**

- Do you clean this machine with oil?*
- **Yes, it's cleaned with oil.**

Ready.

1 Do you wash these clothes in water?*
. . . .
2 Do you cook this fish in oil?*
. . . .
3 Do you grow these plants outside?*
. . . .
4 Do you clean this furniture with wax?*
. . . .
5 Do you wash these dishes in a dishwasher?*
. . . .
6 Do you remove these leaves with a knife?*
. . . .

Unit 13 That's a possibility

Unit 13, Exercise 1

Listen to how these sentences with past modals are pronounced.
"Must have":
– She must have missed the bus.

"Could have":
– She could have forgotten.

Now listen to people talking about why someone missed an appointment. Repeat the sentences. Ready.

1 She must have missed the bus.*
2 She could have forgotten.*
3 She may have had to work overtime.*
4 She might have had another meeting.*
5 She could have changed her mind.*
6 She must have decided not to come.*
7 She could have gone straight home.*
8 She might not have known about it.*

Unit 13, Exercise 2

[*Note:* This conversation is on page 82 of the Student's Book.]

Listen to this conversation.

A: You know, we're studying dinosaurs in science class. It's really interesting.
B: Oh, yeah? Hey, have you learned why the dinosaurs disappeared?
A: Well, no one knows for sure.
B: I thought it had something to do with the climate. The temperature might have gotten cooler and killed them off.
A: Yeah, that's one theory. Another idea is that they may have run out of food.
B: Uh-huh. And you know, there's even a theory that they could have been destroyed by aliens from outer space.
A: That sounds crazy to me!

Now listen and repeat each sentence. Ready.

Unit 13, Exercise 3

You will hear a statement about the cause of a traffic accident, like this:
– The driver was probably drunk.

Reply with "may have," like this:
– **Yes, the driver may have been drunk.**

– The car was probably going too fast.*
– **Yes, the car may have been going too fast.**

Ready.

1 The driver was probably drunk.*
. . . .
2 The car was probably going too fast.*
. . . .
3 The road was probably wet.*
. . . .
4 The brakes were probably not working right.*
. . . .
5 The driver probably fell asleep.*
. . . .
6 The driver probably lost control of the car.*
. . . .

Unit 13, Exercise 4

A man has lost a set of keys and is trying to remember where he left them. Reply to what he says with "could have," like this:
– Maybe I left them at work.*
– **Yes, you could have left them at work.**

Ready.

1 Maybe I dropped them in the subway.*
. . . .
2 Maybe they fell out of my pocket somewhere.*
. . . .
3 Maybe I put them in the kitchen.*
. . . .
4 Maybe I gave them to my assistant.*
. . . .
5 Maybe I left them at home.*
. . . .
6 Maybe I took them to the cafeteria.*
. . . .
Oh, here they are! I found them!

(Unit 13 continues on next page.)

50   Part 2

Unit 13, Exercise 5

Listen to people describing things they did.
Agree with them, like this:
- I found some money on the street. I took it to
  the police station.*
- **I would have taken it to the police
  station too.**

- I lost my wallet, so I put an ad in the paper.*
- **I would have put an ad in the paper too.**
Ready.

1 My sister damaged my car, so I asked her to
  pay for it.*
  . . . .
2 I got very poor service in a restaurant. I
  refused to leave a tip.*
  . . . .
3 My neighbors always make a lot of noise. I
  complained to the building manager.*
  . . . .
4 I saw someone cheat during the test. I spoke
  to the teacher about it.*
  . . . .
5 I forgot my best friend's birthday, so I
  invited her out to dinner.*
  . . . .
6 I had a really unpleasant taxi ride from the
  airport. I complained to the taxi company.*
  . . . .

Unit 13, Exercise 6

Listen to someone talking about a job
interview. Respond like this:
- Do you think I should have asked for a
  higher salary?*
- **No, I don't think you should have asked
  for a higher salary.**

- Do you think I should have said the job
  sounded boring?*
- **No, I don't think you should have said
  the job sounded boring.**

Ready.
1 Do you think I should have asked more
  questions?*
  . . . .
2 Do you think I should have asked to speak to
  the manager?*
  . . . .
3 Do you think I should have asked for an
  air-conditioned office?*
  . . . .
4 Do you think I should have asked for a
  longer vacation?*
  . . . .
5 Do you think I should have tried to make
  jokes during the interview?*
  . . . .
6 Do you think I should have asked for a
  higher salary?*
  . . . .

Unit 13, Exercise 7

Listen to people talking about things they are
going to do. Reply like this:
- I hate my job. I'm going to resign.*
- **I wouldn't resign if I were you.**

- My course is boring. I'm going to drop it.*
- **I wouldn't drop it if I were you.**

Ready.
1 I hate my job. I'm going to resign.*
  . . . .
2 I'm going to change careers.*
  . . . .
3 I'm going to buy a motorcycle.*
  . . . .
4 I'm going to study all night.*
  . . . .
5 I'm going to ask for a higher salary.*
  . . . .
6 I'm going to stop studying English.*
  . . . .

Unit 14 The right stuff

Unit 14, Exercise 1

Listen and combine these statements like this:
A: What does a successful magazine need?
B: To be informative.*
**– A successful magazine needs to be
  informative.**

Listen to another example.
A: What does a successful salesperson need?
B: To be outgoing and persuasive.*
**– A successful salesperson needs to be
  outgoing and persuasive.**

Ready.

1 A: What does a successful TV program need?
   B: To be entertaining and lively.*
. . . .

2 A: What does a successful novel need?
   B: To be well written and interesting.*
. . . .

3 A: What does a successful inventor need?
   B: To be creative and practical.*
. . . .

4 A: What does a successful advertisement
       need?
   B: To be simple and eye-catching.*
. . . .

5 A: What does a successful businessperson
       need?
   B: To be hardworking and tough.*
. . . .

6 A: What does a successful salesperson need?
   B: To be outgoing and persuasive.*
. . . .

Unit 14, Exercise 2

Make sentences with "If you want to be a
writer," like this:
– You have to read a lot.*
**– If you want to be a writer, you have to
  read a lot.**

– You need to have lots of ideas.*
**– If you want to be a writer, you need to
  have lots of ideas.**

Ready.

1 You need to read a lot.*
. . . .

2 You have to be creative.*
. . . .

3 You need to have a good imagination.*
. . . .

4 You should be able to use a word processor.*
. . . .

5 You should have a good understanding of
   people.*
. . . .

Unit 14, Exercise 3

Make sentences with "If you want to be
successful in business," like this:
– You must be dynamic.*
**– If you want to be successful in business,
  you must be dynamic.**

– You need to have a lot of patience.*
**– If you want to be successful in business,
  you need to have a lot of patience.**

Ready.

1 You must be hardworking.*
. . . .

2 You have to take risks.*
. . . .

3 You need to have a lot of ideas.*
. . . .

4 You must be tough.*
. . . .

5 You need to have patience.*
. . . .

(Unit 14 continues on next page.)

Unit 14, Exercise 4

Listen to reporters on a TV news program give opinions about different things. Then answer the question, like this:

– Is the book well written?

WOMAN: The new thriller by John Clancy won't disappoint you. As usual, the story is complex and told with great skill. The characters are memorable, and the dialog is realistic.

– Is the book well written?*

– Yes, it's very well written.

Listen to another example.

– Is the restaurant in a good location?

MAN: You won't want to miss the new Chinese restaurant in the business district, which doesn't get much traffic after 5 o'clock. It looks like the restaurant will have to struggle to attract customers at night.

– Is the restaurant in a good location?*

– No, it's not in a very good location.

Ready.

1 Is the TV program dynamic?

WOMAN: This is one of the most exciting new shows of the season. Each episode has fast-paced adventure and a surprise ending. You won't want to miss one minute.

– Is the TV program dynamic?*

· · · · · · · · · · · · · · · · · · ·

2 Is the gadget practical?

MAN: This gadget is called a "key finder." You attach it to your keys, and it makes a sound so you can find them. It's a good idea, but unfortunately it doesn't make a very loud sound, so it doesn't make finding your keys any easier.

– Is the gadget practical?*

· · · · · · · · · · · · · · · · · · ·

3 Does the shopping center have good parking facilities?

WOMAN: The new shopping center has a store for every need and every budget. But it *doesn't* have a parking space for every car! Long lines of cars and heavy traffic in the parking lot are likely to keep customers away.

– Does the shopping center have good parking facilities?*

· · · · · · · · · · · · · · · · · · ·

4 Does the cafe have a good menu?

MAN: The River Cafe is one place you won't want to miss. It has a small but excellent menu which includes soups, salads, and wonderful desserts. I recommend everything on the menu highly.

– Does the cafe have a good menu?*

· · · · · · · · · · · · · · · · · · ·

5 Does the new park have good sports facilities?

MAN: If you're a tennis player, you'll love the new park – it has eight beautiful tennis courts. But if you like swimming, soccer, and other sports, you're out of luck. I don't know why they built such a nice park with so few sports facilities.

– Does the new park have good sports facilities?*

· · · · · · · · · · · · · · · · · · ·

Unit 14, Exercise 5

[*Note:* This conversation is on page 91 of the Student's Book.]

Listen to this conversation.

A: Look at this interesting ad! What do you think it's advertising?

B: Gee, it looks like an ad for a car.

A: Mmm, try again.

B: Well, it could be an ad for clothes. But whatever it's selling, it's a great photograph.

A: Yeah. It really caught my eye!

Now listen and repeat each sentence. Ready.

Unit 14, Exercise 6

Listen to people talking about different topics. What are they talking about? Listen to this example.
- What are they talking about: a TV program, a book, or a movie?
A: So what did you think?
B: I loved it! The characters were so believable.
A: Yeah, I agree. The acting was fantastic. It was definitely worth the price of admission.
B: Mm-hmm. In fact, I'm ready to go see it again!
- What are they talking about: a TV program, a book, or a movie?*
- **A movie.**

Ready.

1 What are they talking about: a TV program, a book, or a movie?
  A: How'd you like it?
  B: Oh, I didn't want to put it down. It was a wonderful story, and really well written.
  A: Yeah, she's one of my favorite authors.
  - What are they talking about: a TV program, a book, or a movie?*

. . . .

2 What are they talking about: an advertisement, a restaurant, or a TV program?
  A: What do you think of this one?
  B: Well, it's clever, that's for sure. It'll probably help sell a lot of them.
  A: Yeah, it really caught my eye.
  - What are they talking about: an advertisement, a restaurant, or a TV program?*

. . . .

3 What are they talking about: a school, a supermarket, or a shopping center?
  A: Hey, it's really nice here.
  B: Yeah. And there's plenty of parking.
  A: Mm-hmm, and also a lot of nice places to eat. Oh look – this place is having a sale! Let's go in.
  - What are they talking about: a school, a supermarket, or a shopping center?*

. . . .

4 What are they talking about: an advertisement, a TV program, or a book?
  A: Did you see it last night?
  B: No. You know I really love it – the acting's great and it's really well done, but it's on too late at night.
  A: I know what you mean. I tape it on my VCR.
  B: Hey, that's a good idea.
  - What are they talking about: an advertisement, a TV program, or a book?*

. . . .

5 What are they talking about: a school, a shopping center, or a hotel?
  A: Let me show you around.
  B: OK.
  A: You'll see that all the rooms here have a nice view and are quite big.
  B: Oh yes, they're lovely.
  A: They each have a bathroom and two beds.
  B: Mm-hmm. And what other facilities do you have?
  A: We have a swimming pool and two restaurants.
  - What are they talking about: a school, a shopping center, or a hotel?*

. . . .

Unit 15   It's a matter of opinion

Unit 15, Exercise 1

[*Note:* This conversation is on page 94 of the Student's Book.]

Listen to this conversation.

A: How was your vacation?
B: It was OK, but every time I lit up a cigarette, someone asked me to stop smoking. I'm getting sick of all these restrictions! I think we should be able to smoke wherever we like in public.
A: Well, I don't know. Non-smokers have their rights, too, you know. I hate breathing other people's smoke.
B: Mmm. Maybe someday there'll be a smokeless cigarette, and then everyone will be happy.

Now listen and repeat each sentence. Ready.

Unit 15, Exercise 2

Repeat each statement and add a tag question, like this:
– People are friendly around here.*
– **People are friendly around here, aren't they?**

– Parking is difficult here.*
– **Parking is difficult here, isn't it?**

Ready.

1 Parking is difficult here.*
   . . . .
2 People drive dangerously here.*
   . . . .
3 You can't find cheap housing around here.*
   . . . .
4 Taxi drivers here are very polite.*
   . . . .
5 Prices have gone up in the last year.*
   . . . .
6 It's difficult to learn English.*
   . . . .
7 They should clean the sidewalks around here.*
   . . . .

Unit 15, Exercise 3

Listen to people giving opinions. Agree with each statement like this:
– People are very friendly here, aren't they?*
– **Yes, they are.**

– The weather is awful here in the winter, isn't it?*
– **Yes, it is.**

Ready.

1 People are very friendly here, aren't they?*
   . . . .
2 It's expensive to own a car, isn't it?*
   . . . .
3 You can't buy much for ten dollars these days, can you?*
   . . . .
4 Drivers here are very courteous, aren't they?*
   . . . .
5 There aren't any good restaurants around here, are there?*
   . . . .
6 They should really clean up this neighborhood, shouldn't they?*
   . . . .
7 Clothes aren't cheap these days, are they?*
   . . . .

Unit 15, Exercise 4

Choose the word that matches the definition you hear. You will hear the definition two times. Listen to an example:
- Which word is defined: "criticize" or "contradict"?
- To point out the faults of someone or something. To point out the faults of someone or something.
- Which word was defined: "criticize" or "contradict"?*
- **Criticize.**

Ready.

1 Which word is defined: "deny" or "apologize"?
  - To say you are sorry for doing something. To say you are sorry for doing something.
  - Which word was defined: "deny" or "apologize"?*
. . . .
2 Which word is defined: "agree" or "contradict"?
  - To give an opposite opinion about something or someone. To give an opposite opinion about something or someone.
  - Which word was defined: "agree" or "contradict"?*
. . . .
3 Which word is defined: "refuse" or "deny"?
  - To say that something is not true. To say that something is not true.
  - Which word was defined: "refuse" or "deny"?*
. . . .
4 Which word is defined: "apologize" or "refuse"?
  - To say you will not do something that you are asked to do. To say you will not do something that you are asked to do.
  - Which word was defined: "apologize" or @LQ = "refuse"?*
. . . .
5 Which word is defined: "congratulate" or "advise"?
  - To praise someone for success or for a happy event. To praise someone for success or for a happy event.
  - Which word was defined: "congratulate" or "advise"?*
. . . .

Unit 15, Exercise 5

Listen to people giving opinions. Say "positive" or "negative." Ready.

1 WOMAN: I think the city has really improved over the last 20 years. It used to be a very boring place to live, but nowadays there are lots of things to do.
  - Does she have a positive or negative opinion?*
. . . .
2 MAN: I never watch TV because it's not worth it. Most of the programs are a real waste of time.
  - Does he have a positive or negative opinion?*
. . . .
3 WOMAN: I'm glad I came to this school. The teachers are helpful and the courses I'm taking are very useful. I've made a lot of friends here too.
  - Does she have a positive or negative opinion?*
. . . .
4 MAN: I refuse to buy a home computer. Everyone talks about computers these days, but how many people really need one? I mean, most people only use them for playing computer games, so what's the point? I'm perfectly happy with my typewriter.
  - Does he have a positive or negative opinion?*
. . . .
5 WOMAN: I think it's cruel to keep animals in a zoo. Most of the time the animals are kept in small cages, and they don't have anything to do. Animals need to have space to run around.
  - Does she have a positive or negative opinion?*
. . . .

(Unit 15 continues on next page.)

Unit 15, Exercise 6

Listen to two people giving opinions about things. Do they agree or disagree?

1 A: I think military service is a good idea for both men *and* women. It teaches young people discipline and respect.
   B: Yeah, and it also teaches them how to *kill* people. I think it's better for young people to go to college or get a job. That's a better way to learn discipline.
   – Do they agree or disagree?*
. . . .

2 A: I think portable stereos should be banned in public places. I hate having to listen to other people's music when I'm at the beach.
   B: I know what you mean. I hate having to hear rock music in the parks. It certainly would be great if they banned it.
   – Do they agree or disagree?*
. . . .

3 A: I'm glad they're banning smoking on airplanes. It's really bad for everyone's health.
   B: What's the big deal? As long as there's a separate section for smokers, I think it's OK.
   – Do they agree or disagree?*
. . . .

4 A: I don't think tourism is really good for developing countries. It only benefits the people who own hotels and restaurants.
   B: Well, it certainly doesn't benefit the working people. It just creates a few low-paying jobs.
   – Do they agree or disagree?*
. . . .

5 A: I think people with large families shouldn't have to pay taxes. They can't afford it. It costs a fortune to put kids through school these days.
   B: Well, I don't know. Maybe paying taxes will stop people from having large families. After all, the earth is already overpopulated.
   – Do they agree or disagree?*
. . . .

Part 3

Part 3 contains the *complete script* for each exercise. The answers are given in bold type.

Unit 1 That's what friends are for

Unit 1, Exercise 1

You will hear a word, then a statement about Jack, like this:
- easygoing
- Jack always worries about things and gets angry easily.

Then you will hear a question, like this:
- Is Jack easygoing?

Answer the question, like this:
- **No, he isn't easygoing.**

Listen to another example:
- independent
- Jack likes to decide things for himself. He doesn't usually ask other people for help or advice.
- Is Jack independent?*
- **Yes, he's independent.**

Ready.
1 sociable
   - Maria doesn't go out much. She doesn't really enjoy meeting people or making new friends.
   - Is Maria sociable?*
   - **No, she isn't sociable.**
2 emotional
   - You never have to guess how Peter feels. Whether he's excited or sad, he shows his feelings very easily.
   - Is Peter emotional?*
   - **Yes, he's emotional.**
3 generous
   - Anne likes helping people. She often gives her friends gifts, and she enjoys spending money on other people.
   - Is Anne generous?*
   - **Yes, she's generous.**
4 patient
   - Mr. Brown doesn't like waiting for anything. If you're only two minutes late for an appointment, he gets upset.
   - Is Mr. Brown patient?*
   - **No, he isn't patient.**
5 proud
   - Bob talks about himself a lot. In fact, he has a very high opinion of himself.
   - Is Bob proud?*
   - **Yes, he's proud.**

Unit 1, Exercise 2

You are looking for a roommate. Listen to people talking about possible roommates, like this:
- You wouldn't like Maria. She's too quiet.

Respond like this:
- **Oh, that doesn't matter. I like people who are quiet.**

Listen to another example.
- You wouldn't want John. He's too independent.*
- **Oh, that doesn't matter. I like people who are independent.**

Ready.
1 You wouldn't like Claudio. He's too serious.*
   Oh, that doesn't matter. I like people who are serious.
2 You wouldn't want Sonia. She's too easygoing.*
   Oh, that doesn't matter. I like people who are easygoing.
3 You wouldn't like Jack. He's too competitive.*
   Oh, that doesn't matter. I like people who are competitive.
4 You wouldn't want Sandy. She's too ambitious.*
   Oh, that doesn't matter. I like people who are ambitious.
5 You don't want Mary. She's too quiet.*
   Oh, that doesn't matter. I like people who are quiet.

Unit 1, Exercise 3

[*Note:* This conversation is on page 2 of the Student's Book.]

Listen to this conversation.

DAVE: [*phone rings*] Hello?
JIM: Hi. My name's Jim Brady. I'm calling about the ad for a roommate.
DAVE: Oh, yes.
JIM: Are you still looking for someone?
DAVE: Yes, we are.
JIM: Oh, good. I'm really interested.
DAVE: Well, there are four of us, and it's a fairly small house, so we want someone who's easy to get along with.
JIM: Well, I'm pretty easygoing.
DAVE: Great! Can I ask you a few questions?

Now repeat each sentence. Ready.

DAVE: [*phone rings*] Hello?*
JIM: Hi. My name's Jim Brady.* I'm calling about the ad for a roommate.*
DAVE: Oh, yes.*
JIM: Are you still looking for someone?*
DAVE: Yes, we are.*

JIM: Oh, good. I'm really interested.*
DAVE: Well, there are four of us,* and it's a fairly
   small house, so we want someone who's easy to
   get along with.*
JIM: Well, I'm pretty easygoing.*
DAVE: Great! Can I ask you a few questions?*

Unit 1, Exercise 4

Listen to people describe things they don't like.
Answer with "I can't stand them either" or "I don't
like them either," like this:
– I can't stand people who are late.*
– I can't stand them either.

– I don't like people who are moody.*
– I don't like them either.

Ready.
1 I don't like people who blow smoke in my face.*
   I don't like them either.
2 I can't stand people who are selfish.*
   I can't stand them either.
3 I don't like people who are lazy.*
   I don't like them either.
4 I can't stand people who are unreliable.*
   I can't stand them either.
5 I can't stand people who are too emotional.*
   I can't stand them either.
6 I don't like people who are impatient.*
   I don't like them either.

Unit 1, Exercise 5

Listen to a description of different people, like this:
– Mary really wants to be a successful business-
   person. She plans to open a business of her own in
   two years and be a millionaire by the time she's 30.

Then choose the best word to describe the person's
personality, like this:
– Is Mary ambitious or competitive?*
– She's ambitious.

Listen to another example.
– Ted loves going out to meet people. He doesn't like
   to stay at home and be alone.
– Is Ted sociable or shy?*
– He's sociable.

Ready.
1 Fred is the kind of guy who always has to be the
   best in the class. He gets really worried if
   someone does better than him at something.
   – Is Fred competitive or easygoing?*
   – He's competitive.
2 Anna never listens to what other people are trying
   to say. She always interrupts and gives her own
   opinion.
   – Is Anna patient or impatient?*
   – She's impatient.

3 If Susan says something, you can be sure she
   means it. She never arrives late for an
   appointment, and she always does what she
   promises to do.
   – Is Susan reliable or unreliable?*
   – She's reliable.
4 Sam is an unpredictable guy. One day he's all
   smiles and very friendly to people. The next day
   he's very quiet and doesn't want to talk to anyone.
   – Is Sam sociable or moody?*
   – He's moody.
5 Jack only thinks about himself. He hates spending
   money on other people, and he doesn't like helping
   friends, either.
   – Is Jack generous or selfish?*
   – He's selfish.

Unit 1, Exercise 6

You will hear a question and a response, like this:
MAN: When did your family move to England?
WOMAN: When I was in primary school.

Respond like this:
**– Her family moved to England when she was
   in primary school.**

Listen to another example.
WOMAN: When did you learn Spanish?
MAN: While I was in college.*
– He learned Spanish while he was in college.

Ready.
1 WOMAN: When did your parents meet?
   MAN: While they were at university.*
   **His parents met while they were at
   university.**
2 MAN: When did you learn to drive?
   WOMAN: When I was in high school.*
   **She learned to drive when she was in high
   school.**
3 WOMAN: When did you first start learning
      English?
   MAN: When I was in grade school.*
   **He first started learning English when he
   was in grade school.**
4 MAN: When did you learn Japanese?
   WOMAN: While I was living in Japan.*
   **She learned Japanese while she was living in
   Japan.**
5 WOMAN: When did you learn to cook?
   MAN: While I was working in a restaurant.
   **He learned to cook while he was working in
   a restaurant.**
6 WOMAN: When did you get married?
   MAN: While I was working in Brazil.*
   **He got married while he was working in
   Brazil.**

Unit 2 On the job

Unit 2, Exercise 1

Listen to a question comparing two professions. Answer with the second one, like this:
– Who do you think is better paid: a teacher or a lawyer?*
– I think a lawyer is better paid than a teacher.

Listen to another example.
– Which is more interesting: being an accountant or a teacher?*
– I think being a teacher is more interesting than being an accountant.

Ready.
1 Which is more interesting: office work or teaching?*
   I think teaching is more interesting than office work.
2 Which is more challenging: being a journalist or a doctor?*
   I think being a doctor is more challenging than being a journalist.
3 Who has better benefits: a taxi driver or a nurse?*
   I think a nurse has better benefits than a taxi driver.
4 Which do you think is more dangerous: being a pilot or a police officer?*
   I think being a police officer is more dangerous than being a pilot.
5 Who do you think is better paid: a clerk or a construction worker?*
   I think a construction worker is better paid than a clerk.

Unit 2, Exercise 2

Listen to a phrase about a job. Does it describe the best or the worst thing about a job? Respond like this:
– the regular hours*
– The best thing about the job is the regular hours.

– the low salary*
– The worst thing about the job is the low salary.

Ready.
1 the long vacations*
   The best thing about the job is the long vacations.
2 working with pleasant people*
   The best thing about the job is working with pleasant people.
3 traveling to work during rush hour*
   The worst thing about the job is traveling to work during rush hour.
4 working in a nice, quiet office*
   The best thing about the job is working in a nice, quiet office.
5 the low salary*
   The worst thing about the job is the low salary.
6 being able to work at home*
   The best thing about the job is being able to work at home.
7 getting only one week's vacation a year*
   The worst thing about the job is getting only one week's vacation a year.

Unit 2, Exercise 3

[*Note:* This conversation is on page 11 of the Student's Book.]

Listen to this conversation.

A: When did you graduate, Celia?
B: I graduated last year.
A: I see. And what have you been doing since then?
B: Traveling mostly. I love to travel, but now I think it's time for me to get a job.
A: Uh-huh. Are you good at foreign languages?
B: Yes, I think so. I speak French and German, and I can speak a little Russian.
A: Mmm. What kind of job are you looking for?
B: Well, I'd like to have a job where I can use my writing skills. I love working with computers and organizing information. Also, I'd like to work in a large office, so that I'm around other people.
A: OK . . . Well, I think I have the perfect job for you!

Now repeat each sentence. Ready.

A: When did you graduate, Celia?*
B: I graduated last year.*
A: I see. And what have you been doing since then?*
B: Traveling mostly.* I love to travel, but now I think it's time for me to get a job.*
A: Uh-huh. Are you good at foreign languages?*
B: Yes, I think so.* I speak French and German, and I can speak a little Russian.*
A: Mmm. What kind of job are you looking for?*
B: Well, I'd like to have a job where I can use my writing skills.* I love working with computers and organizing information.* Also, I'd like to work in a large office, so that I'm around other people.*
A: OK . . . Well, I think I have the perfect job for you!*

Unit 2, Exercise 4

Listen to a question about abilities, like this:
– How well do you speak French?

Reply like this:
– I speak French pretty well.

Listen to another example.
– How well do you type?*
– I type pretty well.

   Ready.

1 How well do you understand German?*
   I understand German pretty well.
2 How well do you write Spanish?*
   I write Spanish pretty well.
3 How well do you write business letters?*
   I write business letters pretty well.
4 How well do you work under pressure?*
   I work under pressure pretty well.
5 How well do you understand computers?*
   I understand computers pretty well.

Unit 2, Exercise 5

Respond to the questions you hear like this:
– How well do you speak German?*
– I can't speak German very well.

– How well can you translate?*
– I can't translate very well.

Ready.
1 How well can you drive?*
   I can't drive very well.
2 How well can you play the guitar?*
   I can't play the guitar very well.
3 How well can you play tennis?*
   I can't play tennis very well.
4 How well can you type?*
   I can't type very well.
5 How well can you speak Spanish?*
   I can't speak Spanish very well.

Unit 2, Exercise 6

Listen to a question about jobs, like this:
– What kind of job are you looking for?

Then you will hear a phrase, like this:
– meet people

Answer like this:
– I'd like a job where I can meet people.

Listen again.
– What kind of job are you looking for?
– work with computers*
– I'd like a job where I can work with computers.

Ready.
1 What kind of job would you prefer?
   use my languages*
   I'd like a job where I can use my languages.
2 What kind of job are you looking for?
   travel overseas*
   I'd like a job where I can travel overseas.
3 What kind of job would you prefer?
   use my writing skills*
   I'd like a job where I can use my writing skills.
4 What kind of job are you hoping to find?
   learn about marketing*
   I'd like a job where I can learn about marketing.

5 What kind of job would you prefer?
   work outdoors*
   I'd like a job where I can work outdoors.

Unit 2, Exercise 7

You will hear two words or phrases, like this:
– French, Spanish

Make a statement like this:
– I'm good at French, but I'm not very good at Spanish.

Listen to another example.
– writing, speaking in public*
– I'm good at writing, but I'm not very good at speaking in public.

Ready.
1 working on a team, managing people*
   I'm good at working on a team, but I'm not very good at managing people.
2 writing reports, keeping deadlines*
   I'm good at writing reports, but I'm not very good at keeping deadlines.
3 using a computer, typing*
   I'm good at using a computer, but I'm not very good at typing.
4 languages, math*
   I'm good at languages, but I'm not very good at math.
5 meeting people, speaking in public*
   I'm good at meeting people, but I'm not very good at speaking in public.

Unit 3   Destinations

Unit 3, Exercise 1

You will hear statements about different places.
Listen and repeat. Ready.
1 Bali is a beautiful little tropical island.*
2 Carmel is a delightful American seaside resort.*
3 Tokyo is a dynamic modern Japanese city.*
4 Detroit is an old American industrial city.*
5 Sorrento is a charming Italian summer resort.*
6 Barcelona is a delightful old Spanish city.*
7 Kensington is a fashionable London suburb.*
8 Singapore is a clean small southeast Asian country.*

Unit 3, Exercise 2

Listen to a phrase. Then use it in a sentence, like this:
– the weather*
– Tell me about the weather in your hometown.

Then you will hear a reply. Listen to another example.

– industry*
– Tell me about industry in your hometown.
– Oh, there isn't much industry.

Ready.
1 the weather*
   Tell me about the weather in your hometown.
   Oh, the climate is fairly mild.
2 entertainment*
   Tell me about entertainment in your hometown.
   Well, there are plenty of theaters and nightclubs.
3 the cost of living*
   Tell me about the cost of living in your hometown.
   Unfortunately, it's a fairly expensive place to live.
4 the population*
   Tell me about the population in your hometown.
   We have a population of about 50,000.
5 public transportation*
   Tell me about public transportation in your hometown.
   Well, there's a good bus system, but no subway.

Unit 3, Exercise 3

Listen to questions about the weather, like this:
– Do you get much snow in the winter?

If you hear "No," reply like this:
– No, we don't get much snow in the winter.

If you hear "Yes," reply like this:
– Yes, we get a lot of snow in the winter.

Here are two examples.
– Do you get much snow in the winter? No.*
– No, we don't get much snow in the winter.

– Is there much humidity in the summer? Yes.*
– Yes, there's a lot of humidity in the summer.

Ready.
1 Do you get much rain in the summer? No.*
   No, we don't get much rain in the summer.
2 Is there much wind in the winter? Yes.*
   Yes, there's a lot of wind in the winter.
3 Is there much humidity in the winter? Yes.*
   Yes, there's a lot of humidity in the winter.
4 Do you get much rain in the fall? Yes.*
   Yes, we get a lot of rain in the fall.
5 Do you get much snow in January? No.*
   No, we don't get much snow in January.
6 Is there much sun in September? Yes.*
   Yes, there's a lot of sun in September.
7 Do you get much snow in November? No.*
   No, we don't get much snow in November.

Unit 3, Exercise 4

[*Note:* This conversation is on page 16 of the Student's Book.]

Listen to this conversation.

A: I'm thinking about spending my vacation in southeast Asia, but I haven't decided where.
B: Oh? What kind of place are you looking for?
A: Somewhere with good weather, that's quiet and far away from the crowds.
B: Hmm, Phuket might be the place.
A: Phuket? Where's that?
B: In Thailand. It's a beautiful island with excellent beaches. I was there last summer. It's fantastic!
A: Sounds good. But what about the weather?
B: The weather is great. And there are plenty of cheap hotels along the beach.
A: It sounds just like the kind of place I'm looking for.

Now listen and repeat each sentence. Ready.

A: I'm thinking about spending my vacation in southeast Asia, but I haven't decided where.*
B: Oh? What kind of place are you looking for?*
A: Somewhere with good weather, that's quiet and far away from the crowds.*
B: Hmm, Phuket might be the place.*
A: Phuket? Where's that?*
B: In Thailand.* It's a beautiful island with excellent beaches.* I was there last summer.* It's fantastic!*
A: Sounds good.* But what about the weather?*
B: The weather is great.* And there are plenty of cheap hotels along the beach.*
A: It sounds just like the kind of place I'm looking for.*

Unit 3, Exercise 5

You will hear a question about two things, like this:
– Are there many shops and restaurants around here?

Reply like this:
– There are plenty of shops, but there aren't many restaurants.

Listen to another example.
– Are there many guesthouses and hotels in your hometown?*
– There are plenty of guesthouses, but there aren't many hotels.

Ready.
1 Are there many department stores and shopping malls nearby?*
   There are plenty of department stores, but there aren't many shopping malls.
2 Are there many offices and factories in the city?*
   There are plenty of offices, but there aren't many factories.
3 Are there many houses and apartment buildings near the beach?*
   There are plenty of houses, but there aren't many apartment buildings.
4 Are there many buses and taxis at the airport?*
   There are plenty of buses, but there aren't many taxis.

5 Are there many shops and markets in your
hometown?*
**There are plenty of shops, but there aren't
many markets.**

Unit 3, Exercise 6

Listen to people describing places they visited. Do
they have a positive or negative opinion of each
place? Say "positive" or "negative." Listen to an
example.
– It's a crowded place. There are too many people
living there, and there aren't any parks or open
spaces.*
– Negative.

Listen to another example.
– It's a charming little town. It has lots of interesting
shops on the main street, and the weather is very
pleasant.*
– Positive.

Ready.
1 There are hardly any tourist attractions, and
there's not much to do there. There aren't enough
good restaurants either.*
Negative.
2 There's plenty of sightseeing, and the beaches are
very clean. The people are friendly too.*
Positive.
3 There's very little poverty there and very little
unemployment. In fact, the standard of living is
pretty high.*
Positive.
4 There's too much pollution and there's lots of
crime downtown. It's a pretty dangerous place to
live.*
Negative.
5 Finding a place to stay can be pretty tricky. There
are a few big hotels, but they aren't very
comfortable and they are very expensive.*
Negative.

Unit 3, Exercise 7

Listen to two people talking about different places.
Then choose the topic they were talking about.
Listen to an example.
– What is the topic: the people or the climate?
– Yes, it's pretty hot, and very humid. I prefer it in
the winter. It's much cooler then.
– What is the topic: the people or the climate?*
– The climate.

Ready.
1 What is the topic: industry or tourist attractions?
– They produce lots of things there, like cars,
watches, and bicycles. So there are plenty of
jobs, and unemployment is very low.
What is the topic: industry or tourist attractions?*
Industry.

2 What is the topic: crime or shopping?
– You'd better not go out alone at night. And be
careful even during the day. Don't carry a lot of
money with you or wear jewelry in public.
What is the topic: crime or shopping?*
Crime.
3 What is the topic: housing or industry?
– Most of the people live in high-rise apartment
buildings. It's very expensive to buy a house
there, and there is little public housing available.
What is the topic: housing or industry?*
Housing.
4 What is the topic: tourist attractions or
transportation?
– There's an excellent subway system, so it's easy
to get around. There are lots of buses too, and
taxis are very cheap.
What is the topic: tourist attractions or
transportation?*
Transportation.
5 What is the topic: tourist attractions or hotels?
– You should go to the museum. It's very famous.
And there are lots of temples and traditional
buildings, like the hotel in the old part of the
city. The best way to see everything is on foot.
What is the topic: tourist attractions or hotels?*
Tourist attractions.
6 What is the topic: shopping or industry?
– You can get very nice clothes there at
reasonable prices. Electronic items like cameras
and radios are also very good bargains.
What is the topic: shopping or industry?*
Shopping.

Unit 4   What a story!

Unit 4, Exercise 1

Listen to a statement about an event, followed by a
Wh-word, like this:
– There was a bank robbery downtown this morning.
– Where.

Ask a question with the Wh-word, like this:
– *Where* was the bank robbery?

Then you will hear a reply. Listen to another
example.
– There was a traffic accident on the freeway last
night.
– When.*
– *When* was the traffic accident?
– Last night, around 10.

Ready.
1 There was a fire in the Carlyle Hotel on Sunday.
Where.*
***Where* was the fire?**
In the Carlyle Hotel.

2 There was an earthquake in South America yesterday.
When.*
When was the earthquake?
Yesterday morning.
3 A plane crashed yesterday because of engine trouble.
Why.*
Why did the plane crash?
Because of engine trouble.
4 There was a bank robbery on Main Street this morning.
Where.*
Where was the bank robbery?
On Main Street.
5 The robber got away in a stolen car.
How.*
How did the robber get away?
By stealing a car.

Unit 4, Exercise 2

Listen to people talking about news events. What topic are they talking about? Listen to an example, like this:
– What is the topic: an art exhibition or a concert?
– It was very crowded. There were lots of interesting paintings on display. And some of the artists were there to answer questions about their paintings.
– What is the topic: an art exhibition or a concert?*
– An art exhibition.

Ready.
1 What is the topic: a traffic accident or an earthquake?
– It sure was scary! Lots of buildings were damaged and several bridges collapsed. But luckily no one was killed.
What is the topic: traffic accident or an earthquake?*
An earthquake.
2 What is the topic: a fire or a robbery?
– It started about midnight. Most of the hotel guests were asleep. As soon as the alarm went off everybody got out of the building as quickly as they could. Luckily only one floor of the hotel was damaged, and no one was hurt.
What is the topic: a fire or a robbery?*
A fire.
3 What is the topic: a sports event or a concert?
– There must have been about 20,000 people there – it was a huge crowd. Unfortunately the visiting team played really well that day. They won 25 to nothing.
What is the topic: a sports event or a concert?*
A sports event.
4 What is the topic: a robbery or a lottery?
– I was really surprised when I learned I had won $25,000. I don't know what I'll do with the money. Maybe I'll take a trip around the world.
What is the topic: a robbery or a lottery?*
A lottery.

5 What is the topic: a storm or a drought?
– It was one of the worst ones we had this year. The wind was very strong and it rained for three days. Lots of trees were blown over, and many houses were damaged.
What is the topic: a storm or a drought?*
A storm.

Unit 4, Exercise 3

Reply to each question about a news event like this:
– Did you hear about the fire downtown?*
– No, I didn't know there was a fire downtown.

Ready.
1 Did you hear about the fire downtown?*
No, I didn't know there was a fire downtown.
2 Did you hear about the earthquake in California?*
No, I didn't know there was an earthquake in California.
3 Did you hear about the party at City Hall last night?*
No, I didn't know there was a party at City Hall last night.
4 Did you hear about the accident on the freeway?*
No, I didn't know there was an accident on the freeway.
5 Did you hear about the fight at the rock concert?*
No, I didn't know there was a fight at the rock concert.

Unit 4, Exercise 4

Listen to people describe things that happened to them. Respond like this:
– Someone ran into my car!*
– Someone ran into your car? When did that happen?

Then you will hear a reply, like this:
– This morning.

Respond like this:
– That's too bad.

Listen to another example.
– I got fired from my job.*
– You got fired from your job? When did that happen?
– Yesterday.*
– That's too bad.

Ready.
1 I lost my wallet.*
You lost your wallet? When did that happen?
This morning.*
That's too bad.
2 Someone broke into my apartment.*
Someone broke into your apartment? When did that happen?
Over the weekend.*
That's too bad.

3 I lost my keys.*
You lost your keys? When did that happen?
On Tuesday, I think.*
That's too bad.
4 I got stopped for speeding.*
You got stopped for speeding? When did that happen?
This morning.*
That's too bad.
5 I had a car accident.*
You had a car accident? When did that happen?
On Sunday.*
That's too bad.

Unit 4, Exercise 5

[*Note:* This conversation is on page 25 of the Student's Book.]

Listen to this conversation.

A: You know, I had a really strange dream last night.
B: Oh yeah? What was it about?
A: Well, I dreamed that I was driving in the country late at night when I saw a UFO land on the road in front of me.
B: And then what happened?
A: Well, first, I got out of my car. While I was standing there, this strange green creature came out of the UFO. I tried to run away, but I couldn't move. Then, as it was coming nearer, it put out its hand and touched my face. It felt wet and horrible!
B: Ugh! And . . . ?
A: And then I woke up and found my cat on my pillow. It was licking my face!

Now repeat each sentence. Ready.

A: You know, I had a really strange dream last night.*
B: Oh, yeah? What was it about?*
A: Well, I dreamed that I was driving in the country late at night* when I saw a UFO land on the road in front of me.*
B: And then what happened?*
A: Well, first, I got out of my car.* While I was standing there, this strange green creature came out of the UFO.* I tried to run away, but I couldn't move.* Then, as it was coming nearer, it put out its hand and touched my face.* It felt wet and horrible!*
B: Ugh! And . . . ?*
A: And then I woke up and found my cat on my pillow.* It was licking my face!*

Unit 4, Exercise 6

Answer these questions about a traffic accident with the second choice, like this:
– Was your friend driving or were you driving the car?*
– I was driving the car.

Ready.

1 Was your friend driving or were you driving the car?*
I was driving the car.
2 Was it a clear night or was it raining?*
It was raining.
3 Were you talking to your friend or were you paying attention to the road?*
I was paying attention to the road.
4 Was the car in front of you making a right turn or a left turn?*
It was making a left turn.
5 Were you speeding up or slowing down?*
I was slowing down.
6 Were you driving without a seat belt or were you wearing a seat belt?*
I was wearing a seat belt.

Unit 4, Exercise 7

Listen to a statement, like this:
– Something interesting happened while I was driving to work today.

Ask what happened, like this:
– Really? What happened while you were driving to work?

Then you will hear a response. Listen to another example.
– Something interesting happened while I was shopping.*
– Really? What happened while you were shopping?
– I saw someone shoplifting.

Ready.

1 Something exciting happened when I was walking downtown.*
Really? What happened when you were walking downtown?
I saw a movie star.
2 Something interesting happened while I was waiting at the airport.*
Really? What happened while you were waiting at the airport?
I saw the President.
3 Something interesting happened when I was coming home on the bus.*
Really? What happened when you were coming home on the bus?
The bus broke down and we had to walk a mile for help.
4 Something interesting happened while I was swimming this morning.*
Really? What happened while you were swimming?
I found a diamond ring at the bottom of the pool.
5 Something embarrassing happened while I was taking a shower.*
Really? What happened while you were taking a shower?
My dinner guests arrived!

Unit 5   Could you do me a favor?

Unit 5, Exercise 1

Make a request using "Could you" and "Please," like this:
– Open the window.*
– **Could you open the window, please?**

Then you will hear a reply. Listen to another example.
– Pass me that book.*
– **Could you pass me that book, please?**
– Yes, here you are.

Ready.
1 Take these books to the library.*
   Could you take these books to the library, please?
   Sure. I'll do it this afternoon.
2 Help me with this exercise.*
   Could you help me with this exercise, please?
   Sure. What's the problem?
3 Give me a ride home after class.*
   Could you give me a ride home after class, please?
   I'm sorry, but I didn't drive my car today.
4 Change a one-hundred dollar bill for me.*
   Could you change a one-hundred dollar bill for me, please?
   Sorry, I don't have change for a hundred dollars.
5 Lend me your car on Saturday.*
   Could you lend me your car on Saturday, please?
   No way. The last time you borrowed my car you had an accident!
6 Mail these letters for me.*
   Could you mail these letters for me, please?
   OK. I'll mail them after class.
7 Let me use your dictionary.*
   Could you let me use your dictionary, please?
   Yeah. Help yourself.

Unit 5, Exercise 2

Make a request using "Would you mind," like this:
– Close the window.*
– **Would you mind closing the window?**

Then listen to the reply. Listen to another example.
– Type this letter for me.*
– **Would you mind typing this letter for me?**
– Sorry, I can't type.

Ready.
1 Lend me fifty dollars.*
   Would you mind lending me fifty dollars?
   No, you still owe me twenty-five dollars from last week!
2 Drive me to the airport.*
   Would you mind driving me to the airport?
   OK. What time do you need to leave?

3 Lend me your class notes.*
   Would you mind lending me your class notes?
   No problem. Here you are.
4 Help me prepare this report.*
   Would you mind helping me prepare this report?
   OK. As soon as I finish typing this letter.
5 Let me use your phone.*
   Would you mind letting me use your phone?
   OK. It's in the hallway.

Unit 5, Exercise 3

Listen to people making requests. Did the second speaker agree or refuse? Listen to this example.
A: I wonder if I could borrow your car on Sunday.
B: Well, actually, I have to take my sister to the airport. Sorry.
– Did the second speaker agree or refuse?*
– **Refuse.**

Ready.
1 A: Could you lend me this magazine for the weekend?
   B: No problem. I'm finished with it. It has some really interesting articles.
   Did the second speaker agree or refuse?*
   Agree.
2 A: I wonder if you'd be able to help me move into my new apartment on Saturday.
   B: Well, I'm not doing much this weekend. What time do you want me to come over?
   Did the second speaker agree or refuse?*
   Agree.
3 A: I wonder if you'd be able to help me with my class project on Thursday night.
   B: Gee, I wish I could, but Thursday night is when I have my karate class.
   Did the second speaker agree or refuse?*
   Refuse.
4 A: Would you mind turning off the TV?
   B: Well, I'm waiting for the news. I want to find out what's happening in the elections.
   Did the second speaker agree or refuse?*
   Refuse.
5 A: Would you be able to read my essay for me and see if I made any mistakes?
   B: Well, I'd really love to read your essay, but I haven't finished my homework yet. Why don't you ask Maria?
   Did the second speaker agree or refuse?*
   Refuse.

Unit 5, Exercise 4

Listen to people ask you to do something. Politely refuse, like this:
– I wonder if you'd mind taking me to the airport tonight.*
– **Oh, I'm sorry. I can't take you to the airport tonight.**

Ready.

1 I wonder if you'd mind taking me to the airport tonight.*
   Oh, I'm sorry. I can't take you to the airport tonight.
2 I wonder if you'd mind typing these letters.*
   Oh, I'm sorry. I can't type these letters.
3 I wonder if you'd mind taking these books back to the library.*
   Oh, I'm sorry. I can't take these books back to the library.
4 I wonder if you'd mind checking my homework.*
   Oh, I'm sorry. I can't check your homework.
5 I wonder if you'd mind lending me your car.*
   Oh, I'm sorry. I can't lend you my car.
6 I wonder if you'd mind lending me fifty dollars.*
   Oh, I'm sorry. I can't lend you fifty dollars.
7 I wonder if you'd mind helping me with my homework.*
   Oh, I'm sorry. I can't help you with your homework.

Unit 5, Exercise 5

[*Note:* This conversation is on page 31 of the Student's Book.]

Listen to this conversation.

A: Hello?
B: Hello. Can I speak to Sophia, please?
A: I'm sorry, she's not in right now. Would you like to leave a message?
B: Yes, please. This is Harry. Would you tell her that Tony's having a party on Saturday?
A: Sure.
B: And please ask her if she'd like to go with me.
A: All right, Peter. I'll give her the message.
B: No, this is Harry, not Peter!
A: Oh, sorry.
B: By the way, who's Peter?

Now repeat each sentence. Ready.

A: Hello?*
B: Hello. Can I speak to Sophia, please?*
A: I'm sorry, she's not in right now.* Would you like to leave a message?*
B: Yes, please. This is Harry.* Would you tell her that Tony's having a party on Saturday?*
A: Sure.*
B: And please ask her if she'd like to go with me.*
A: All right, Peter. I'll give her the message.*
B: No, this is Harry, not Peter!*
A: Oh, sorry.*
B: By the way, who's Peter?*

Unit 5, Exercise 6

Ask someone to give messages to Sue, like this:
– Jack's having a party tonight.*
– Could you tell Sue that Jack's having a party tonight?

Listen to another example.
– There's a tennis game on Saturday.*
– Could you tell Sue that there's a tennis game on Saturday?

Ready.
1 The meeting tomorrow has been canceled.*
   Could you tell Sue that the meeting tomorrow has been canceled?
2 There's a letter for her in the office.*
   Could you tell Sue that there's a letter for her in the office?
3 Don't be late for our appointment.*
   Could you tell Sue not to be late for our appointment?
4 I'll call her at 9 p.m. tomorrow.*
   Could you tell Sue that I'll call her at 9 p.m. tomorrow?
5 There's an interesting movie playing downtown.*
   Could you tell Sue that there's an interesting movie playing downtown?
6 Don't forget to return the money she borrowed.*
   Could you tell Sue not to forget to return the money she borrowed?

Unit 6 Comparatively speaking

Unit 6, Exercise 1

Answer the questions with the second choice, like this:
– Would you rather learn the piano or the guitar?*
– I'd rather learn the guitar.

– Would you rather live in a house or an apartment?*
– I'd rather live in an apartment.

Ready.
1 Would you rather live in the city or in the suburbs?*
   I'd rather live in the suburbs.
2 Would you rather study at a large or a small university?*
   I'd rather study at a small university.
3 Would you rather have a motorcycle or a car?*
   I'd rather have a car.
4 Would you rather travel by air or by train?*
   I'd rather travel by train.
5 Would you rather send your children to a public school or a private school?*
   I'd rather send my children to a private school.
6 Would you rather live in a house or an apartment?*
   I'd rather live in an apartment.

Unit 6, Exercise 2

Ask a question with "Would rather," like this:
– work outdoors or indoors*
– Would you rather work outdoors or indoors?

Then you will hear a reply. Listen to another example.
– listen to classical music or pop music*
– Would you rather listen to classical music or pop music?
– Oh, I prefer classical music.

Ready.
1 work outdoors or indoors*
   Would you rather work outdoors or indoors?
   I'd rather work outdoors.
2 see a movie in a theater or rent a video*
   Would you rather see a movie in a theater or rent a video?
   Mmm . . . I'd rather rent a video.
3 study English in Australia or Canada*
   Would you rather study English in Australia or Canada?
   Australia, I think, because it's warmer there.
4 learn the guitar or the piano*
   Would you rather learn the guitar or the piano?
   I'd rather learn the piano.
5 be a teacher or an actor*
   Would you rather be a teacher or an actor?
   I'd rather be a teacher, I think.
6 work for someone else or be self-employed*
   Would you rather work for someone else or be self-employed?
   That's easy! I'd rather be self-employed.

Unit 6, Exercise 3

Answer each question with the second choice. Then ask a follow-up question, like this:
– Do you prefer studying part-time or full-time?*
– I prefer studying full-time. How about you?

Then you will hear a response. Listen to another example.
– Do you prefer reading or watching TV?*
– I prefer watching TV. How about you?
– Oh, I prefer reading.

Ready.
1 Do you prefer studying part-time or full-time?*
   I prefer studying full-time. How about you?
   So do I.
2 Do you prefer studying in a large class or a small class?*
   I prefer studying in a small class. How about you?
   So do I.
3 Do you prefer playing tennis or golf?*
   I prefer playing golf. How about you?
   I do too.
4 Do you prefer swimming at the beach or in a pool?*
   I prefer swimming in a pool. How about you?
   Well, I prefer the beach.
5 Do you prefer reading novels or magazines?*
   I prefer reading magazines. How about you?
   I like them both.

6 Do you prefer traveling by ship or by air?*
   I prefer traveling by air. How about you?
   Not me. I prefer traveling by ship.

Unit 6, Exercise 4

[*Note:* This conversation is on page 34 of the Student's Book.]

Listen to this conversation.

ANN: Would you rather send your children to a public or a private school?
TOM: Mmm, I'd rather send them to a public school, I think.
ANN: Oh, why?
TOM: Well, it's cheaper for one thing . . .
ANN: Yes, but do you think the teachers are as good in the public schools?
TOM: Oh, yeah, I went to a public high school, and I had very good teachers there.

Now repeat each sentence. Ready.

ANN: Would you rather send your children to a public or a private school?*
TOM: Mmm, I'd rather send them to a public school, I think.*
ANN: Oh, why?*
TOM: Well, it's cheaper for one thing . . . *
ANN: Yes, but do you think the teachers are as good in the public schools?*
TOM: Oh, yeah, I went to a public high school,* and I had very good teachers there.*

Unit 6, Exercise 5

Answer the questions with the first choice. Then ask a follow-up question, like this:
– Is your sister teaching at an elementary school or a secondary school?*
– She's teaching at an elementary school. Where is your sister teaching?

Then you will hear a response. Listen to another example.
– Do you go to a public school or a private school?*
– I go to a public school. Where do you go?
– I go to a public school too.

Ready.
1 Are you studying at a technical college or a university?*
   I'm studying at a technical college. Where are you studying?
   I'm not studying anymore. I graduated last month.
2 Does your brother teach at a community college or a high school?*
   He teaches at a community college. Where does your brother teach?
   He teaches at a high school.
3 Are you studying literature or philosophy?*
   I'm studying literature. What are you studying?
   I'm studying physics.

4 Do you have classes in the daytime or in the evening?*
   I have classes in the daytime. When do you have classes?
   I have both daytime *and* evening classes.
5 Do you teach at a high school or a technical school?*
   I teach at a high school. Where do you teach?
   I teach first grade at an elementary school.

Unit 6, Exercise 6

Answer the questions like this:
– Do a lot of students go to school until they're 16 here?*
– Yes, in fact most students go to school until they're 16 here.

– Do a lot of colleges teach French?*
– Yes, in fact most colleges teach French.

Ready.
1 Do a lot of students go to school until they're 16 here?*
   Yes, in fact most students go to school until they're 16 here.
2 Do a lot of colleges teach French?*
   Yes, in fact most colleges teach French.
3 Do a lot of students take English in high school?*
   Yes, in fact most students take English in high school.
4 Do a lot of teachers have a college degree?*
   Yes, in fact most teachers have a college degree.
5 Do a lot of colleges have dorms?*
   Yes, in fact most colleges have dorms.
6 Do a lot of students finish high school?*
   Yes, in fact most students finish high school.

Unit 6, Exercise 7

Listen to statements about education. Ask for clarification by repeating each statement, like this:
– Very few schools teach Korean.*
– Did you say that very few schools teach Korean?

Then you will hear a reply. Listen to another example.
– Neither teachers nor students wear uniforms.*
– Did you say that neither teachers nor students wear uniforms?
– That's right.

Ready.
1 Not many schools have language labs.*
   Did you say that not many schools have language labs?
   Yes, that's right.
2 Not all primary schools teach English.*
   Did you say that not all primary school teach English?
   Yes, I did.

3 A few schools have Saturday classes.*
   Did you say that a few schools have Saturday classes?
   Yes, that's what I said.
4 Both elementary schools and high schools have large classes.*
   Did you say that both elementary schools and high schools have large classes?
   Yes, they both have large classes.
5 None of the private schools is cheap.*
   Did you say that none of the private schools is cheap?
   Yes, in fact they're quite expensive.
6 Most high schools don't have school uniforms.*
   Did you say that most high schools don't have school uniforms?
   Yes, although some private high schools do.

Unit 7   Don't drink the water

Unit 7, Exercise 1

Practice saying consonant clusters with /s/. Listen and repeat. Ready.
1 The cost of the trip includes plane tickets and bus trips.*
2 The flight to the east coast lasts for three hours and fifty minutes.*
3 The next flight leaves in just a few minutes.*
4 My father often makes trips to the bookshops to buy old books.*
5 There are lots of interesting ships down at the docks.*
6 A good journalist collects facts first and then writes.*

Unit 7, Exercise 2

Listen to a phrase, like this:
– to see old cities

Use it to complete this sentence:
– Many people visit Europe.

Listen to two examples:
– to see old cities*
– Many people visit Europe to see old cities.

– to shop*
– Many people visit Europe to shop.

Ready.
1 to enjoy the food*
   Many people visit Europe to enjoy the food.
2 to see the museums and churches*
   Many people visit Europe to see the museums and churches.
3 to buy clothes*
   Many people visit Europe to buy clothes.
4 to see the old cities*
   Many people visit Europe to see the old cities.

5 to practice a foreign language.*
Many people visit Europe to practice a foreign language.

Unit 7, Exercise 3

Report what each person says, like this:
WOMAN: I'm going to Spain. I want to learn Spanish.*
– She's going to Spain so she can learn Spanish.

MAN: I'm going to London. I want to find a job there.*
– He's going to London so he can find a job there.

Ready.
1 MAN: I'm going to Paris. I want to learn French.*
He's going to Paris so he can learn French.
2 WOMAN: I'm going to Los Angeles. I want to go to a friend's wedding.*
She's going to Los Angeles so she can go to a friend's wedding.
3 MAN: I'm going to Switzerland. I want to do some skiing.*
He's going to Switzerland so he can do some skiing.
4 WOMAN: I'm going to Florida. I want to visit Disney World.*
She's going to Florida so she can visit Disney World.
5 MAN: I'm going to Australia. I want to go camping.*
He's going to Australia so he can go camping.

Unit 7, Exercise 4

[*Note:* This conversation is on page 42 of the Student's Book.]

Listen to this conversation.

A: I'm thinking of going to Brazil next year, Maria.
B: Oh, great! I'm sure you'll have a good time.
A: What places do tourists visit in Brazil?
B: Well, a lot of people go to Rio for Carnival. And nowadays, lots of people are visiting the Amazon to take river trips.
A: Oh, really? That sounds interesting. And when's a good time to visit?
B: Well, I like Rio in the spring or fall because it's not too hot then.

Now repeat each sentence. Ready.

A: I'm thinking of going to Brazil next year, Maria.*
B: Oh, great! I'm sure you'll have a good time.*
A: What places do tourists visit in Brazil?*
B: Well, a lot of people go to Rio for Carnival.* And nowadays, lots of people are visiting the Amazon to take river trips.*
A: Oh, really? That sounds interesting.* And when's a good time to visit?*
B: Well, I like Rio in the spring or fall because it's not too hot then.*

Unit 7, Exercise 5

Report each person's reasons with "because of," like this:
WOMAN: I don't like Hong Kong. There's too much pollution.*
– She doesn't like Hong Kong because of the pollution.

MAN: I like living in Italy. I really love the food.*
– He likes living in Italy because of the food.

Ready.
1 WOMAN: I like Brazil. The people are wonderful.*
She likes Brazil because of the people.
2 MAN: I enjoy living in Los Angeles. It has great nightlife.*
He enjoys living in Los Angeles because of the nightlife.
3 WOMAN: I like traveling in Asia. The hotels are excellent.*
She likes traveling in Asia because of the hotels.
4 WOMAN: I love Washington, D.C. It has fantastic museums.*
She loves Washington, D.C., because of the museums.
5 MAN: I don't like Europe in the summer. There are too many tourists.*
He doesn't like Europe in the summer because of the tourists.
6 MAN: I love Italy. The food is great.*
He loves Italy because of the food.

Unit 7, Exercise 6

Listen to people talk about different places. They say some good points and *one* problem. What problem do they mention? Listen to an example:
WOMAN: I loved my vacation in Thailand. The beaches were fantastic and the hotels were reasonably priced. Unfortunately it was very crowded because it was tourist season.
– What problem does she mention?*
– It was very crowded.

Listen to another example.
MAN: I enjoyed my trip a lot. The city had excellent museums, and I enjoyed the theater too. There was only one drawback: It wasn't safe at night. I had to be careful.
– What problem does he mention?*
– It wasn't safe at night.

Ready.
1 WOMAN: You have to visit Madrid. It's a wonderful city. I especially liked the nightlife – they have wonderful clubs and discos. I loved everything except the cars. Madrid has very heavy traffic. But the people are warm and friendly, and I can't wait to go back.
– What problem does she mention?*
It has very heavy traffic.

2 MAN: I went to a small town in the mountains for my vacation. It was very quiet and relaxing. No TV, no movies, just nature. That's the way I like it. But it's hard to enjoy yourself when there's terrible poverty all around you.
– What problem does he mention?*
There was terrible poverty.

3 WOMAN: I stayed with friends last weekend. We had a good time, even though the buses and trains were on strike! We had to stay home because it was too hard to get anywhere in the city. So we just played some tennis, watched videos, and visited.
– What problem does she mention?*
The buses and trains were on strike.

4 MAN: I just got back from Washington, D.C. You know, I went there to visit the museums and do some research for school. The museums were excellent, and the subway system was very clean and easy to use. My only disappointment was that the art gallery I wanted to visit was closed. They were doing some repairs.
– What problem does he mention?*
The art gallery he wanted to visit was closed.

5 WOMAN: My trip to Tokyo was incredible. The only bad thing I have to say is that my trip was too short! My hotel was excellent, the sightseeing was very interesting, and the people were really helpful and polite.
– What problem does she mention?*
The trip was too short.

Unit 7, Exercise 7

You are talking to someone about customs in their country. Ask questions with "What happens when . . ." like this:
– You are invited to someone's house for dinner.*
– What happens when you are invited to someone's house for dinner?

Then you will hear a reply. Listen to another example.
– You meet someone for the first time.*
– What happens when you meet someone for the first time?
– Oh, you generally shake hands.

Ready.
1 You are invited to someone's house for dinner.*
What happens when you are invited to someone's house for dinner?
You usually bring a gift, like flowers or a bottle of wine.
2 You go out to dinner with friends.*
What happens when you go out to dinner with friends?
You usually share the bill.
3 Your friend is going to have a baby.*
What happens when your friend is going to have a baby?
Well, you have a party for her and give her gifts.

4 You make an appointment with someone.*
What happens when you make an appointment with someone?
You should arrive on time.
5 A friend has a birthday party.*
What happens when a friend has a birthday party?
You usually take a card, and perhaps a small gift.
6 You stay at someone's home.*
What happens when you stay at someone's home?
It's nice to give them a gift, and also help out around the house.

Unit 8   Getting things done

Unit 8, Exercise 1

Ask where you can get things done, like this:
– a passport photo taken*
– Do you know where I could get a passport photo taken?

Then you will hear a reply. Listen to another example.
– my hair cut*
– Do you know where I could get my hair cut?
– Sure. There's a barber down the street, at the corner.

Ready.
1 a camera repaired*
Do you know where I could get a camera repaired?
Sure. You can get it repaired at the camera shop in the mall.
2 my shoes repaired*
Do you know where I could get my shoes repaired?
No, I'm not really sure. Sorry.
3 color photocopies made*
Do you know where I could get color photocopies made?
I think there's a place on Fourth Street.
4 my stereo fixed*
Do you know where I could get my stereo fixed?
Try the electronics store on Main Street.
5 a typewriter fixed*
Do you know where I could get a typewriter fixed?
No, I don't. Why don't you look in the phone book?
6 my car serviced*
Do you know where I could get my car serviced?
Well, Danny's Auto Shop on Fourth Street is *my* favorite place.

Unit 8, Exercise 2

Listen to a guest at a hotel say things that need to be done, like this:
– I need to have these shoes repaired.

You are the hotel clerk. Reply like this:
– Oh, I'll have them repaired for you.

Listen to another example.
– I need to have this suit cleaned.*
– Oh, I'll have it cleaned for you.

Ready.
1 I need to have these shoes repaired.*
 Oh, I'll have them repaired for you.
2 I need to have this suit cleaned.*
 Oh, I'll have it cleaned for you.
3 I need to have this film developed.*
 Oh, I'll have it developed for you.
4 I need to have this fax sent.*
 Oh, I'll have it sent for you.
5 I need to have this report typed.*
 Oh, I'll have it typed for you.

Unit 8, Exercise 3

Practice the sounds /s/ and /sh/. Listen and repeat these sentences. Ready.
1 I'm looking for a store that sells washing machines.*
2 Should I have these silk shirts washed or dry cleaned?*
3 You can use this machine to get cash.*
4 It's not expensive to get your shoes shined on the street.*
5 I bought these sheets at a special sale on Saturday.*
6 My hair is a mess, so I'm getting it cut and shampooed.*

Unit 8, Exercise 4

[*Note:* This conversation is on page 51 of the Student's Book.]

Listen to this conversation.

A: I've got a friend coming for the weekend who loves jazz. Where's a good place to take her?
B: Uh, why not take her to the New Orleans Club? That's a great place to hear live music.
C: Yeah, but it's hard to get in on the weekend. I like the Back Door better because it's not so crowded.
A: Oh, yeah? Do they have dancing there?
C: Uh, I don't think so.

Now repeat each sentence. Ready.

A: I've got a friend coming for the weekend who loves jazz.* Where's a good place to take her?*

B: Uh, why not take her to the New Orleans Club?* That's a great place to hear live music.*
C: Yeah, but it's hard to get in on the weekend.* I like the Back Door better because it's not so crowded.*
A: Oh, yeah? Do they have dancing there?*
C: Uh, I don't think so.*

Unit 8, Exercise 5

Listen to a phrase like this:
– hear live music

Ask a question using "Where's a good place to," like this:
– hear live music*
– Where's a good place to hear live music?

Listen to the reply, and then repeat the location and thank the speaker, like this:
– At the disco.*
– At the disco? OK, thanks.

Listen to the whole example again.
– hear live music*
– Where's a good place to hear live music?
– At the disco.*
– At the disco? OK, thanks.

Listen to another example.
– buy fresh seafood*
– Where's a good place to buy fresh seafood?
– At the fish market downtown.*
– At the fish market downtown? OK, thanks.

Ready.
1 buy CDs*
 Where's a good place to buy CDs?
 There's a good music store at the mall.*
 At the mall? OK, thanks.
2 have Italian food*
 Where's a good place to have Italian food?
 There's a great Italian restaurant in the Park Hotel.*
 In the Park Hotel? OK, thanks.
3 buy books*
 Where's a good place to buy books?
 There's a good bookstore near the university.*
 Near the university? OK, thanks.
4 try local food*
 Where's a good place to try local food?
 Try the restaurants in the Old Town.*
 In the Old Town? OK, thanks.
5 buy interesting souvenirs*
 Where's a good place to buy interesting souvenirs?
 Try the market near the train station.*
 Near the train station? OK, thanks.
6 see interesting architecture*
 Where's a good place to see interesting architecture?
 The best place is around City Hall.*
 Around City Hall? OK, thanks.

Unit 8, Exercise 6

Listen to a question. Then you will hear someone describing a place. Answer the question, like this:
- What is she describing: a disco, a library, or a bank?
FEMALE: It's always busy. A lot of tourists go there to change traveler's checks. And of course it's in the business district, so a lot of businesses have accounts there. But the service is quick and efficient, and the tellers are very friendly.
- What is she describing: a disco, a library, or a bank?*
- **A bank.**

Ready.
1 What is she describing: a bank, a restaurant, or a market?
  FEMALE: I like it there. Everything is really cheap, and the quality is pretty good too. Plus it's lively, so it's a fun place to shop.
  - What is she describing: a bank, a restaurant, or a market?*
  A market.
2 What is he describing: a beach, an airport, or a building?
  MALE: It's one of my favorite places in the city. It's over 500 years old and was designed by a very famous architect. It's open to the public during the week but not on weekends.
  - What is he describing: a beach, an airport, or a building?*
  A building.
3 What is she describing: a bookstore, a railway station, or a supermarket?
  WOMAN: It's probably the best of its kind in town. I like it because there is a large English section. And the salespeople are great. They let you spend as much time as you want reading. They don't pressure you to buy.
  - What is she describing: a bookstore, a railway station, or a supermarket?*
  A bookstore.
4 What is he describing: a supermarket, a music store, or a cafe?
  MALE: I often drop in there after class to get a bite to eat or to meet friends. They usually have live music there in the evenings.
  - What is he describing: a supermarket, a music store, or a cafe?*
  A cafe.
5 What is she describing: a restaurant, a park, or a store?
  FEMALE: It's a nice place to go and relax. It's quiet and very pretty in the summer, when all the flowers are out. Lots of people go there to eat their lunch when the weather is nice.
  - What is she describing: a restaurant, a park, or a store?*
  A park.

Unit 8, Exercise 7

Answer questions about different places, like this:
- Is the nightclub noisy?*
- **No, I like it because it's not so noisy.**

- Is the beach crowded?*
- **No, I like it because it's not so crowded.**

Ready.
1 Is the park usually crowded?*
  No, I like it because it's not so crowded.
2 Is the jazz club expensive?*
  No, I like it because it's not so expensive.
3 Is the New Orleans Club very noisy?*
  No, I like it because it's not so noisy.
4 Is the swimming pool very deep?*
  No, I like it because it's not so deep.
5 Is the bookstore usually busy?*
  No, I like it because it's not so busy.

Unit 9 Is that a fact?

Unit 9, Exercise 1

You will hear four numbers. What year do they describe? Listen and say the year, like this:
- 1, 9, 2, 3*
- **The year nineteen twenty-three.**

- 1, 5, 0, 0*
- **The year fifteen hundred.**

Ready.
1 1, 9, 2, 3*
  The year nineteen twenty-three.
2 1, 5, 0, 0*
  The year fifteen hundred.
3 1, 8, 9, 6*
  The year eighteen ninety-six.
4 1, 9, 6, 9*
  The year nineteen sixty-nine.
5 1, 7, 0, 5*
  The year seventeen-O-five.
6 2, 0, 0, 1*
  The year two thousand and one.

Unit 9, Exercise 2

You will hear an event like this:
- the first flight in a jumbo jet

Ask a question with "When was . . . ," like this:
- **When was the first flight in a jumbo jet?**

Then you will hear a reply. Listen to another example.
- the first satellite launched*
- **When was the first satellite launched?**
- In the late fifties, I believe.

Ready.
1 the first flight in a jumbo jet*
When was the first flight in a jumbo jet?
In 1970.
2 the first subway opened*
When was the first subway opened?
In 1863.
3 the first compact disc sold*
When was the first compact disc sold?
In 1983.
4 the first color movie shown*
When was the first color movie shown?
I think it was in 1930.
5 plastic invented*
When was plastic invented?
In 1909.
6 the first personal computer sold*
When was the first personal computer sold?
In 1975.

Unit 9, Exercise 3

Listen to a statement about a past event, like this:
– World War One began.

Ask a question with "When did," like this:
– When did World War One begin?

Then you will hear the answer. Listen to another example.
– World War Two ended.*
– When did World War Two end?
– In 1945.

Ready.
1 World War One began.*
When did World War One begin?
In 1914.
2 The first person traveled in space.*
When did the first person travel in space?
In 1961.
3 Jazz first became popular.*
When did jazz first become popular?
In the 1920s.
4 George Orwell published the novel *1984*.*
When did George Orwell publish the novel *1984*?
In 1949.
5 The French Revolution began.*
When did the French Revolution begin?
In 1789.
6 Japan began trading with China.*
When did Japan begin trading with China?
In the year 606.

Unit 9, Exercise 4

[*Note:* This conversation is on page 57 of the Student's Book.]

Listen to this conversation.

A: I've just been reading an interesting article about robots. Did you know that the typical factory worker in the future will be a robot?

B: Really? That's scary.
A: Yeah, and they'll even use robots to make and repair other robots.
B: That's hard to imagine. And when is this supposed to happen?
A: Within thirty years. And robots will also be building factories in outer space and even mining minerals on the moon.
B: Hey, maybe by then they'll have invented a robot to clean my apartment!

Now listen and repeat each sentence. Ready.

A: I've just been reading an interesting article about robots.* Did you know that the typical factory worker in the future will be a robot?*
B: Really? That's scary.*
A: Yeah, and they'll even use robots to make and repair other robots.*
B: That's hard to imagine.* And when is this supposed to happen?*
A: Within thirty years.* And robots will also be building factories in outer space* and even mining minerals on the moon.*
B: Hey, maybe by then they'll have invented a robot to clean my apartment!*

Unit 9, Exercise 5

Listen to a phrase. Then ask questions about what will happen in five years, like this:
– living in the same place*
– Do you think you'll be living in the same place in five years?

Then you will hear a reply. Listen to another example.
– have the same friends*
– Do you think you'll have the same friends in five years?
– No, I'll probably have lots of new friends in five years.

Ready.
1 be living in the same place*
Do you think you'll be living in the same place in five years?
I hope not.
2 have the same job*
Do you think you'll have the same job in five years?
Yes, probably. I like my job.
3 be driving the same car*
Do you think you'll be driving the same car in five years?
Probably not. My car is already 15 years old!
4 look any different*
Do you think you'll look any different in five years?
I'd rather not think about it.
5 dress any differently*
Do you think you'll dress any differently in five years?
I'm not sure.

6 own your own home*
Do you think you'll own your home in five years?
I hope so.

Unit 9, Exercise 6

Listen to predictions about the year 2050. Disagree by making a negative statement, like this:
– People will be living on the moon.*
– Oh, I don't think people will be living on the moon.

– They will have discovered a cure for cancer.*
– Oh, I don't think they will have discovered a cure for cancer.

Ready.
1 People will be living on the moon.*
Oh, I don't think people will be living on the moon.
2 They will have discovered a cure for cancer.*
Oh, I don't think they will have discovered a cure for cancer.
3 They will have discovered a way to prevent aging.*
Oh, I don't think they will have discovered a way to prevent aging.
4 People will be driving electric cars.*
Oh, I don't think people will be driving electric cars.
5 Cities will be built under the ocean.*
Oh, I don't think cities will be built under the ocean.
6 They will have found a cure for baldness.*
Oh, I don't think they will have found a cure for baldness.
7 Everyone will be speaking English.*
Oh, I don't think everyone will be speaking English.

Unit 10   There's no place like home

Unit 10, Exercise 1

Reply to questions about household chores, like this:
– Do you like washing dishes?*
– No, I can't stand washing dishes. How about you?

Then you will hear a reply. Listen to another example.
– Do you like vacuuming?*
– No, I can't stand vacuuming. How about you?
– I can't stand it either.

Ready.
1 Do you like cleaning bathrooms?*
No, I can't stand cleaning bathrooms. How about you?
I can't stand it either.

2 Do you like scrubbing floors?*
No, I can't stand scrubbing floors. How about you?
Oh, I don't mind it once in a while.
3 Do you like ironing clothes?*
No, I can't stand ironing clothes. How about you?
Oh, it's OK, I guess.
4 Do you like doing laundry?*
No, I can't stand doing laundry. How about you?
I'm not crazy about it either.
5 Do you like washing dishes?*
No, I can't stand washing dishes. How about you?
Oh, I enjoy it.
6 Do you like cleaning the yard?*
No, I can't stand cleaning the yard. How about you?
I like it. I enjoy being outside.

Unit 10, Exercise 2

Answer questions about a house or an apartment, like this:
– Does it have a kitchen and a laundry room?*
– It has a kitchen, but it doesn't have a laundry room.

– Does it have a patio and a yard?*
– It has a patio, but it doesn't have a yard.

Ready.
1 Does it have a living room and a dining room?*
It has a living room, but it doesn't have a dining room.
2 Does it have a garden and a pool?*
It has a garden, but it doesn't have a pool.
3 Does it have a yard and a patio?*
It has a yard, but it doesn't have a patio.
4 Does it have central heating and air conditioning?*
It has central heating, but it doesn't have air conditioning.
5 Does it have a balcony and a view?*
It has a balcony, but it doesn't have a view.
6 Does it have a bathtub and a shower?*
It has a bathtub, but it doesn't have a shower.

Unit 10, Exercise 3

Answer the questions you hear about a town or neighborhood, like this:
– Is there a good bus system and a subway?*
– Yes, there's a good bus system as well as a subway.

– Is there a shopping mall and a market?*
– Yes, there's a shopping mall as well as a market.

Ready.
1 Is there an elementary school and a high school?*
Yes, there's an elementary school as well as a high school.

2 Is there a park and a public swimming pool?*
   **Yes, there's a park as well as a public
   swimming pool.**
3 Is there a gas station and a supermarket?*
   **Yes, there's a gas station as well as a
   supermarket.**
4 Is there a taxi stand and a bus stop?*
   Yes, there's a taxi stand as well as a bus stop.
5 Is there a bank and a post office?*
   Yes, there's a bank as well as a post office.
6 Is there a shopping mall and a department store?*
   **Yes, there's a shopping mall as well as a
   department store.**

Unit 10, Exercise 4

[*Note:* This conversation is on page 62 of the
Student's Book.]

Listen to this conversation.

A: Have you moved to your new apartment yet, Fred?
B: Yes, we moved in last Saturday.
A: So, how do you like it?
B: Oh, it's great! There's plenty of room, and it's
    quiet too.
A: Yeah? Uh, what's the building like? Does it have
    a pool?
B: No, it doesn't have a pool, but there's a patio
    downstairs and a big yard for the kids to play in.
A: It sounds nice.
B: It is. Why don't you come over this weekend and
    see it?
A: OK. I'd like to.

Now repeat each sentence. Ready.

A: Have you moved to your new apartment yet,
    Fred?*
B: Yes, we moved in last Saturday.*
A: So, how do you like it?*
B: Oh, it's great!* There's plenty of room, and it's
    quiet too.*
A: Yeah? Uh, what's the building like? Does it have
    a pool?*
B: No, it doesn't have a pool,* but there's a patio
    downstairs and a big yard for the kids to play in.*
A: It sounds nice.*
B: It is. Why don't you come over this weekend and
    see it?*
A: OK. I'd like to.*

Unit 10, Exercise 5

Answer questions about a neighborhood, like this:
– Is there a shopping mall and a department store?*
**– There's no shopping mall, although there's a
department store.**

– Is there a movie theater and a good video store?*
**– There's no movie theater, although there's a
good video store.**

Ready.

1 Is there a subway and a good bus system?*
   **There's no subway, although there's a good
   bus system.**
2 Is there a park and a public swimming pool?*
   **There's no park, although there's a public
   swimming pool.**
3 Is there a shopping center and a market?*
   **There's no shopping center, although there's
   a market.**
4 Is there a restaurant and a fast food store?*
   **There's no restaurant, although there's a fast
   food store.**
5 Is there a post office and a bank?*
   **There's no post office, although there's a
   bank.**
6 Is there a bookstore and a library?*
   **There's no bookstore, although there's a
   library.**

Unit 10, Exercise 6

Listen to people talking to their apartment manager
about problems in their apartment. Reply with the
second choice, like this:
– What's the problem? Is it the bedroom fan or the
kitchen fan?*
– It's the *kitchen* fan.

Pay attention to stress. Listen to another example.
– What's the problem? Is it the bathroom window or
the bedroom window?*
– It's the *bedroom* window.

Ready.
1 What's the problem? Is it the bedroom fan or the
   kitchen fan?*
   It's the *kitchen* fan.
2 Which one is stuck? Is it the bathroom window or
   the bedroom window?*
   It's the *bedroom* window.
3 What's wrong? Is it the kitchen light or the
   bathroom light?*
   It's the *bathroom* light.
4 Where's the leak? Is it the hot water faucet or the
   cold water faucet?*
   It's the *cold water* faucet.
5 Which one is broken? Is it the living room air
   conditioner or the bedroom air conditioner?*
   It's the *bedroom* air conditioner.
6 Which door needs repairing? Is it the front door or
   the back door?*
   It's the *back* door.
7 Which telephone doesn't work? Is it the one in the
   bedroom or the one in the kitchen?*
   It's the one in the *kitchen*.

Unit 10, Exercise 7

Listen to people talking about a problem with
something in their apartment. Listen and say what
they are talking about, like this.
– Is she talking about the TV, the lamp, or the iron?

WOMAN: I noticed that the room was getting darker. Then it started to make a strange buzzing sound. So I unplugged it and called a repairperson immediately.
– Is she talking about the TV, the lamp, or the iron?*
– The lamp.

Ready.

1 Is she talking about the stove, the refrigerator, or the air conditioner?
   WOMAN: Something's definitely wrong. It's not cooling properly. The food that I put in it yesterday was spoiled by today.
   – Is she talking about the stove, the refrigerator, or the air conditioner?*
   The refrigerator.

2 Is he talking about the radio, the television, or the telephone?
   MAN: It's been out of order for several hours. I can't get a dial tone. I'd like to get it fixed as soon as possible because I have to make some important business calls.
   – Is he talking about the radio, the television, or the telephone?*
   The telephone.

3 Is he talking about the bedroom, the living room, or the kitchen?
   MAN: I wish you could fix the central heating in there. When I go to bed at night it's so cold that I can't get to sleep.
   – Is he talking about the bedroom, the living room, or the kitchen?*
   The bedroom.

4 Is she talking about the stove, the dryer, or the central heating?
   WOMAN: It hasn't been heating right for some time. Sometimes it gets too hot and burns everything. Other times it doesn't get hot enough, and things don't get cooked.
   – Is she talking about the stove, the dryer, or the central heating?*
   The stove.

5 Is he talking about the central heating, the lamp, or the air conditioner?
   MAN: It's been driving me crazy all summer! It keeps breaking down and it doesn't keep the room cool. It's so hot in this room most of the time that I can hardly breathe.
   – Is he talking about the central heating, the lamp, or the air conditioner?*
   The air conditioner.

Unit 11   What a world we live in!

Unit 11, Exercise 1

[*Note:* This conversation is on page 68 of the Student's Book.]

Listen to this conversation.

A: Did you hear that Jerry lost his job?
B: Oh, he did? Gee, that's too bad.
A: Yeah, the company wasn't making money, so they had to lay off some employees.
B: So what's Jerry going to do now?
A: Well, he's thinking of starting his own business.
B: Oh, that's great. I don't know what I'd do if I lost my job. Maybe I'd go back to school. What would you do?
A: Well, first I think I'd probably take a vacation. After that, I guess I'd try working for myself too.

Now repeat each sentence. Ready.

A: Did you hear that Jerry lost his job?*
B: Oh, he did? Gee, that's too bad.*
A: Yeah, the company wasn't making money,* so they had to lay off some employees.*
B: So what's Jerry going to do now?*
A: Well, he's thinking of starting his own business.*
B: Oh, that's great.* I don't know what I'd do if I lost my job.* Maybe I'd go back to school.* What would you do?*
A: Well, first I think I'd probably take a vacation.* After that, I guess I'd try working for myself too.*

Unit 11, Exercise 2

You will hear a situation. Ask a question using "What would you do?" like this:
– Suppose you lost your job.*
– What would you do if you lost your job?

Then you will hear a reply. Listen to another example.
– Suppose you became president of your country.*
– What would you do if you became president of your country?
– I'd give everyone a job.

Ready.

1 Suppose you lost your job.*
   What would you do if you lost your job?
   I'd look for another one.
2 Suppose you won the lottery.*
   What would you do if you won the lottery?
   I'd start my own business.
3 Suppose someone asked you for a big loan.*
   What would you do if someone asked you for a big loan?
   I'd tell them to go to a bank.
4 Suppose you found a lot of money on the street.*
   What would you do if you found a lot of money on the street?
   I'd take it to the police.
5 Suppose you could start your own business.*
   What would you do if you could start your business?
   I'd open a restaurant.
6 Suppose you could live in a foreign country.*
   What would you do if you could live in a foreign country?
   I'd move to Alaska.

Unit 11, Exercise 3

Listen to people saying what they would do if they
won a million dollars. Report what they say like this:
WOMAN: What would I do? Buy a boat and sail
around the world.*
– She'd buy a boat and sail around the world.

MAN: What would I do? Marry my childhood
sweetheart.*
– He'd marry his childhood sweetheart.

Ready.
1 WOMAN: What would I do? Buy a boat and sail
around the world.*
She'd buy a boat and sail around the world.
2 MAN: What would I do? Move to California and
become an artist.*
He'd move to California and become an artist.
3 MAN: What would I do? Give it all away.*
He'd give it all away.
4 WOMAN: What would I do? Stop working and go
back to school.*
She'd stop working and go back to school.
5 MAN: What would I do? Buy myself a house and a
car.*
He'd buy himself a house and a car.
6 WOMAN: What would I do? Go into politics and
run for mayor.*
She'd go into politics and run for mayor.

Unit 11, Exercise 4

Practice these sentences with plural "s." Listen and
repeat. Ready.
1 Families in apartments shouldn't keep pets.*
2 Drivers who have large cars should pay higher
taxes.*
3 Workers in government offices receive good
benefits.*
4 It often takes weeks to answer letters from friends
and relatives.*
5 Students with overdue library books must pay a
fine of ten dollars.*

Unit 11, Exercise 5

Listen to two people talking, like this:
A: What if the government raised taxes?
B: People would complain.

Report what they say, like this:
**– If the government raised taxes, people would
complain.**

Listen to another example.
A: What if employers raised salaries?
B: People would spend more.*
**– If employers raised salaries, people would
spend more.**

Ready.
1 A: What if the government raised taxes?
B: People would complain.*

**If the government raised taxes, people would
complain.**
2 A: What if people had smaller families?
B: We might need fewer schools.*
**If people had smaller families, we might
need fewer schools.**
3 A: What if cars were banned in cities?
B: There would be less pollution.*
**If cars were banned in cities, there would be
less pollution.**
4 A: What if everyone spoke English well?
B: There would be no jobs for English teachers.*
**If everyone spoke English well, there would
be no jobs for English teachers.**
5 A: What if banks charged lower interest rates?
B: More people could buy homes.*
**If banks charged lower interest rates, more
people could buy homes.**

Unit 11, Exercise 6

Someone is talking to you about problems in a
country you have visited recently. Answer the
questions like this:
– Is reducing the air pollution a problem there?*
– Yes, reducing air pollution is a real problem.

– Is controlling drugs a problem there?*
– Yes, controlling drugs is a real problem.

Ready.
1 Is reducing air pollution a problem there?*
Yes, reducing air pollution is a real problem.
2 Is keeping drugs off the streets a problem there?*
**Yes, keeping drugs off the streets is a real
problem.**
3 Is finding cheap housing a problem there?*
Yes, finding cheap housing is a real problem.
4 Is controlling traffic noise a problem there?*
**Yes, controlling traffic noise is a real
problem.**
5 Is finding jobs for graduates a problem there?*
**Yes, finding jobs for graduates is a real
problem.**
6 Is making the cities safer a problem there?*
Yes, making the cities safer is a real problem.
7 Is reducing unemployment a problem there?*
**Yes, reducing unemployment is a real
problem.**

Unit 11, Exercise 7

Listen to people giving opinions. What topics are
they talking about? Listen to an example.
– What is she talking about: pollution, inflation, or
traffic?
WOMAN: I wish we had a subway system in this city.
I can't stand driving to work anymore. You know,
it's only a 15-minute drive, but during rush hour
it takes me an *hour*.
– What is she talking about: pollution, inflation, or
traffic?*
– Traffic.

Ready.
1 What is he talking about: pollution, inflation, or traffic?
   MAN: It's really time the government did something about it. It's not only the air we breathe that's so bad. It's also the beaches. The water isn't clean enough to swim in anymore. It's a shame.
   – What is he talking about: pollution, inflation, or traffic?*
   Pollution.
2 What is she talking about: employment, crime, or public housing?
   WOMAN: I don't go out alone at night anymore. I don't think it's safe. And I never leave my car parked downtown. Otherwise it's likely to get stolen.
   – What is she talking about: employment, crime, or public housing?*
   Crime.
3 What is he talking about: noise, poverty, or traffic?
   MAN: It's OK if you leave before 6 o'clock in the morning to drive to work. But if you leave any later than that it's impossible to get to work on time. I hate to say it, but we need to build more freeways. It's getting more and more difficult to drive from one side of the city to the other during rush hours.
   – What is he talking about: noise, poverty, or traffic?*
   Traffic.
4 What is she talking about: education, unemployment, or inflation?
   WOMAN: The situation seems to be getting worse. More and more students find there is no job waiting for them when they graduate. And more and more people are losing their jobs too.
   – What is she talking about: education, unemployment, or inflation?*
   Unemployment.
5 What is she talking about: crime, drugs, or smoking?
   WOMAN: These days it's banned almost everywhere: in most public places, in the workplace, even on airplanes. It's just not fair. A little smoke never hurt anyone.
   – What is she talking about: crime, drugs, or smoking?*
   Smoking.

Unit 12   How does it work?

Unit 12, Exercise 1

[*Note:* This conversation is on page 74 of the Student's Book.]

Listen to this conversation.

A: Are you good at crossword puzzles?
B: Well, sometimes.

A: OK. What's this? It's a small piece of curved wire that's used for holding sheets of paper together.
B: Gee, I have no idea.
A: All right. Then how about this one? This instrument, which is usually made of metal or plastic, is used for eating food. It has a handle at one end and two or more points at the other.
B: I'm sorry. I can't guess that one either.

Now listen and repeat each sentence. Ready.

A: Are you good at crossword puzzles?*
B: Well, sometimes.*
A: OK. What's this?* It's a small piece of curved wire that's used for holding sheets of paper together.*
B: Gee, I have no idea.*
A: All right. Then how about this one?* This instrument, which is usually made of metal or plastic,* is used for eating food.* It has a handle at one end* and two or more points at the other.*
B: I'm sorry. I can't guess that one either.*

Unit 12, Exercise 2

Make a sentence using "that," like this:
– a machine for cleaning floors*
– It's a machine that's used for cleaning floors.

– a liquid for cleaning glass*
– It's a liquid that's used for cleaning glass.

Ready.
1 a tool for cutting wire*
   It's a tool that's used for cutting wire.
2 a container for holding liquids*
   It's a container that's used for holding liquids.
3 a utensil for cutting paper*
   It's a utensil that's used for cutting paper.
4 a gadget for opening bottles*
   It's a gadget that's used for opening bottles.
5 a machine for cleaning carpets*
   It's a machine that's used for cleaning carpets.
6 a tool for chopping wood*
   It's a tool that's used for chopping wood.

Unit 12, Exercise 3

Ask a question with "What's the stuff that's used" and the phrase you hear, like this:
– to stick things together*
– What's the stuff that's used to stick things together?

Then you will hear a reply. Listen to another example.
– to polish floors*
– What's the stuff that's used to polish floors?
– Oh, that's called wax.

Ready.

1 to clean shoes*
What's the stuff that's used to clean shoes?
Oh, that's shoe polish.
2 to clean your teeth*
What's the stuff that's used to clean your teeth?
It's called toothpaste.
3 used to make plants grow*
What's the stuff that's used to make plants grow?
It's called fertilizer.
4 used to wash clothes*
What's the stuff that's used to wash clothes?
Oh, that's detergent.
5 to stick things together*
What's the stuff that's used to stick things together?
It's called glue.
6 to clean wood*
What's the stuff that's used to clean wood?
It's called polish.

Unit 12, Exercise 4

Answer the questions you hear with the second choice, like this:
– Are you looking for the cassette player or the tape recorder?*
– The *tape* recorder.

Pay attention to stress. Listen to another example.
– Are you looking for the coffee machine or the rice cooker?*
– The *rice* cooker.

Ready.
1 Are you looking for the paper clips or the letter opener?*
The *letter* opener.
2 Are you looking for the bookshelf or the coffee table?*
The *coffee* table.
3 Are you looking for the swimming pool or the tennis court?*
The *tennis* court.
4 Are you looking for the pencil sharpener or the paper clips?*
The *paper* clips.
5 Are you looking for the letter opener or the pocket knife?*
The *pocket* knife.
6 Are you looking for the floor polish or the soap powder?*
The *soap* powder.

Unit 12, Exercise 5

Answer each question with the first choice, like this:
– Are tires usually made of rubber or plastic?*
– They're usually made of rubber.

– Are windows usually made of glass or plastic?*
– They're usually made of glass.

Ready.
1 Are soft contact lenses usually made of plastic or glass?*
They're usually made of plastic.
2 Are shoes usually made of leather or rubber?*
They're usually made of leather.
3 Are coins usually made of metal or plastic?*
They're usually made of metal.
4 Are bottles usually made of glass or steel?*
They're usually made of glass.
5 Are carpets usually made of wool or cotton?*
They're usually made of wool.

Unit 12, Exercise 6

Listen to people asking about things that need to be done and reply like this:
– Do you want me to clean the living room?*
– Yes, it needs to be cleaned.

– Do you want me to wash the dishes?*
– Yes, they need to be washed.

Ready.
1 Do you want me to clean the living room?*
Yes, it needs to be cleaned.
2 Do you want me to wash the dishes?*
Yes, they need to be washed.
3 Do you want me to water the plants?*
Yes, they need to be watered.
4 Do you want me to take out the garbage?*
Yes, it needs to be taken out.
5 Do you want me to iron the clothes?*
Yes, they need to be ironed.

Unit 12, Exercise 7

Listen to someone asking for information. Reply like this.
– Do you grow these plants inside?*
– Yes, they're grown inside.

– Do you clean this machine with oil?*
– Yes, it's cleaned with oil.

Ready.
1 Do you wash these clothes in water?*
Yes, they're washed in water.
2 Do you cook this fish in oil?*
Yes, it's cooked in oil.
3 Do you grow these plants outside?*
Yes, they're grown outside.
4 Do you clean this furniture with wax?*
Yes, it's cleaned with wax.
5 Do you wash these dishes in a dishwasher?*
Yes, they're washed in a dishwasher.
6 Do you remove these leaves with a knife?*
Yes, they're removed with a knife.

Unit 13   That's a possibility

Unit 13, Exercise 1

Listen to how these sentences with past modals are pronounced.
"Must have":
– She must have missed the bus.

"Could have":
– She could have forgotten.

Now listen to people talking about why someone missed an appointment. Repeat the sentences. Ready.
1   She must have missed the bus.*
2   She could have forgotten.*
3   She may have had to work overtime.*
4   She might have had another meeting.*
5   She could have changed her mind.*
6   She must have decided not to come.*
7   She could have gone straight home.*
8   She might not have known about it.*

Unit 13, Exercise 2

[*Note:* This conversation is on page 82 of the Student's Book.]

Listen to this conversation.

A: You know, we're studying dinosaurs in science class. It's really interesting.
B: Oh, yeah? Hey, have you learned why the dinosaurs disappeared?
A: Well, no one knows for sure.
B: I thought it had something to do with the climate. The temperature might have gotten cooler and killed them off.
A: Yeah, that's one theory. Another idea is that they may have run out of food.
B: Uh-huh. And you know, there's even a theory that they could have been destroyed by aliens from outer space.
A: That sounds crazy to me!

Now listen and repeat each sentence. Ready.

A: You know, we're studying dinosaurs in science class.* It's really interesting.*
B: Oh, yeah?* Hey, have you learned why the dinosaurs disappeared?*
A: Well, no one knows for sure.*
B: I thought it had something to do with the climate.* The temperature might have gotten cooler and killed them off.*
A: Yeah, that's one theory.* Another idea is that they may have run out of food.*
B: Uh-huh.* And you know, there's even a theory that they could have been destroyed by aliens from outer space.*
A: That sounds crazy to me!*

Unit 13, Exercise 3

You will hear a statement about the cause of a traffic accident, like this:
– The driver was probably drunk.

Reply with "may have," like this:
– **Yes, the driver may have been drunk.**

– The car was probably going too fast.*
– **Yes, the car may have been going too fast.**

Ready.
1   The driver was probably drunk.*
    Yes, the driver may have been drunk.
2   The car was probably going too fast.*
    Yes, the car may have been going too fast.
3   The road was probably wet.*
    Yes, the road may have been wet.
4   The brakes were probably not working right.*
    Yes, the brakes may not have been working right.
5   The driver probably fell asleep.*
    Yes, the driver may have fallen asleep.
6   The driver probably lost control of the car.*
    Yes, the driver may have lost control of the car.

Unit 13, Exercise 4

A man has lost a set of keys and is trying to remember where he left them. Reply to what he says with "could have," like this:
– Maybe I left them at work.*
– **Yes, you could have left them at work.**

Ready.
1   Maybe I dropped them in the subway.*
    Yes, you could have dropped them in the subway.
2   Maybe they fell out of my pocket somewhere.*
    Yes, they could have fallen out of your pocket somewhere.
3   Maybe I put them in the kitchen.*
    Yes, you could have put them in the kitchen.
4   Maybe I gave them to my assistant.*
    Yes, you could have given them to your assistant.
5   Maybe I left them at home.*
    Yes, you could have left them at home.
6   Maybe I took them to the cafeteria.*
    Yes, you could have taken them to the cafeteria.
    Oh, here they are! I found them!

Unit 13, Exercise 5

Listen to people describing things they did. Agree with them, like this:
– I found some money on the street. I took it to the police station.*
– **I would have taken it to the police station too.**

– I lost my wallet, so I put an ad in the paper.*
– **I would have put an ad in the paper too.**

Ready.
1 My sister damaged my car, so I asked her to pay for it.*
   I would have asked her to pay for it too.
2 I got very poor service in a restaurant. I refused to leave a tip.*
   I would have refused to leave a tip too.
3 My neighbors always make a lot of noise. I complained to the building manager.*
   I would have complained to the building manager too.
4 I saw someone cheat during the test. I spoke to the teacher about it.*
   I would have spoken to the teacher about it too.
5 I forgot my best friend's birthday, so I invited her out to dinner.*
   I would have invited her out to dinner too.
6 I had a really unpleasant taxi ride from the airport. I complained to the taxi company.*
   I would have complained to the taxi company too.

Unit 13, Exercise 6

Listen to someone talking about a job interview. Respond like this:
– Do you think I should have asked for a higher salary?*
– No, I don't think you should have asked for a higher salary.

– Do you think I should have said the job sounded boring?*
– No, I don't think you should have said the job sounded boring.

Ready.
1 Do you think I should have asked more questions?*
   No, I don't think you should have asked more questions.
2 Do you think I should have asked to speak to the manager?*
   No, I don't think you should have asked to speak to the manager.
3 Do you think I should have asked for an air-conditioned office?*
   No, I don't think you should have asked for an air-conditioned office.
4 Do you think I should have asked for a longer vacation?*
   No, I don't think you should have asked for a longer vacation.
5 Do you think I should have tried to make jokes during the interview?*
   No, I don't think you should have tried to make jokes during the interview.
6 Do you think I should have asked for a higher salary?*
   No, I don't think you should have asked for a higher salary.

Unit 13, Exercise 7

Listen to people talking about things they are going to do. Reply like this:
– I hate my job. I'm going to resign.*
– I wouldn't resign if I were you.

– My course is boring. I'm going to drop it.*
– I wouldn't drop it if I were you.

Ready.
1 I hate my job. I'm going to resign.*
   I wouldn't resign if I were you.
2 I'm going to change careers.*
   I wouldn't change careers if I were you.
3 I'm going to buy a motorcycle.*
   I wouldn't buy a motorcycle if I were you.
4 I'm going to study all night.*
   I wouldn't study all night if I were you.
5 I'm going to ask for a higher salary.*
   I wouldn't ask for a higher salary if I were you.
6 I'm going to stop studying English.*
   I wouldn't stop studying English if I were you.

Unit 14 The right stuff

Unit 14, Exercise 1

Listen and combine these statements like this:
A: What does a successful magazine need?
B: To be informative.*
– A successful magazine needs to be informative.

Listen to another example.
A: What does a successful salesperson need?
B: To be outgoing and persuasive.*
– A successful salesperson needs to be outgoing and persuasive.

Ready.
1 A: What does a successful TV program need?
   B: To be entertaining and lively.*
   A successful TV program needs to be entertaining and lively.
2 A: What does a successful novel need?
   B: To be well written and interesting.*
   A successful novel needs to be well written and interesting.
3 A: What does a successful inventor need?
   B: To be creative and practical.*
   A successful inventor needs to be creative and practical.
4 A: What does a successful advertisement need?
   B: To be simple and eye-catching.*
   A successful advertisement needs to be simple and eye-catching.
5 A: What does a successful businessperson need?
   B: To be hardworking and tough.*
   A successful businessperson needs to be hardworking and tough.

6 A: What does a successful salesperson need?
   B: To be outgoing and persuasive.*
   **A successful salesperson needs to be
   outgoing and persuasive.**

Unit 14, Exercise 2

Make sentences with "If you want to be a writer,"
like this:
– You have to read a lot.*
**– If you want to be a writer, you have to read a
lot.**

– You need to have lots of ideas.*
**– If you want to be a writer, you need to have
lots of ideas.**

Ready.
1 You need to read a lot.*
   **If you want to be a writer, you need to read
   a lot.**
2 You have to be creative.*
   **If you want to be a writer, you have to be
   creative.**
3 You need to have a good imagination.*
   **If you want to be a writer, you need to have
   a good imagination.**
4 You should be able to use a word processor.*
   **If you want to be a writer, you should be
   able to use a word processor.**
5 You should have a good understanding of people.*
   **If you want to be a writer, you should have a
   good understanding of people.**

Unit 14, Exercise 3

Make sentences with "If you want to be successful in
business," like this:
– You must be dynamic.*
**– If you want to be successful in business, you
must be dynamic.**

– You need to have a lot of patience.*
**– If you want to be successful in business, you
need to have a lot of patience.**

Ready.
1 You must be hardworking.*
   **If you want to be successful in business, you
   must be hardworking.**
2 You have to take risks.*
   **If you want to be successful in business, you
   have to take risks.**
3 You need to have a lot of ideas.*
   **If you want to be successful in business, you
   need to have a lot of ideas.**
4 You must be tough.*
   **If you want to be successful in business, you
   must be tough.**
5 You need to have patience.*
   **If you want to be successful in business, you
   need to have patience.**

Unit 14, Exercise 4

Listen to reporters on a TV news program give
opinions about different things. Then answer the
question, like this:
– Is the book well written?
WOMAN: The new thriller by John Clancy won't
   disappoint you. As usual, the story is complex and
   told with great skill. The characters are
   memorable, and the dialog is realistic.
– Is the book well written?*
– Yes, it's very well written.

Listen to another example.
– Is the restaurant in a good location?
MAN: You won't want to miss the new Chinese
   restaurant in the business district, which doesn't
   get much traffic after 5 o'clock. It looks like the
   restaurant will have to struggle to attract
   customers at night.
– Is the restaurant in a good location?*
– No, it's not in a very good location.

Ready.
1 Is the TV program dynamic?
   WOMAN: This is one of the most exciting new
      shows of the season. Each episode has
      fast-paced adventure and a surprise ending.
      You won't want to miss one minute.
   – Is the TV program dynamic?*
   Yes, it's very dynamic.
2 Is the gadget practical?
   MAN: This gadget is called a "key finder." You
      attach it to your keys, and it makes a sound so
      you can find them. It's a good idea, but
      unfortunately it doesn't make a very loud
      sound, so it doesn't make finding your keys
      any easier.
   – Is the gadget practical?*
   No, it's not very practical.
3 Does the shopping center have good parking
   facilities?
   WOMAN: The new shopping center has a store for
      every need and every budget. But it *doesn't*
      have a parking space for every car! Long lines
      of cars and heavy traffic in the parking lot are
      likely to keep customers away.
   – Does the shopping center have good parking
   facilities?*
   **No, it doesn't have very good parking
   facilities.**
4 Does the cafe have a good menu?
   MAN: The River Cafe is one place you won't want
      to miss. It has a small but excellent menu
      which includes soups, salads, and wonderful
      desserts. I recommend everything on the menu
      highly.
   – Does the cafe have a good menu?*
   Yes, it has a very good menu.
5 Does the new park have good sports facilities?
   MAN: If you're a tennis player, you'll love the new
      park – it has eight beautiful tennis courts. But
      if you like swimming, soccer, and other sports,

you're out of luck. I don't know why they built such a nice park with so few sports facilities.
– Does the new park have good sports facilities?*
No, it doesn't have very good sports facilities.

Unit 14, Exercise 5

[*Note:* This conversation is on page 91 of the Student's Book.]

Listen to this conversation.

A: Look at this interesting ad! What do you think it's advertising?
B: Gee, it looks like an ad for a car.
A: Mmm, try again.
B: Well, it could be an ad for clothes. But whatever it's selling, it's a great photograph.
A: Yeah. It really caught my eye!

Now listen and repeat each sentence. Ready.

A: Look at this interesting ad!* What do you think it's advertising?*
B: Gee, it looks like an ad for a car.*
A: Mmm, try again.*
B: Well, it could be an ad for clothes.* But whatever it's selling, it's a great photograph.*
A: Yeah. It really caught my eye!*

Unit 14, Exercise 6

Listen to people talking about different topics. What are they talking about? Listen to this example.
– What are they talking about: a TV program, a book, or a movie?
A: So what did you think?
B: I loved it! The characters were so believable.
A: Yeah, I agree. The acting was fantastic. It was definitely worth the price of admission.
B: Mm-hmm. In fact, I'm ready to go see it again!
– What are they talking about: a TV program, a book, or a movie?*
– A movie.

Ready.
1 What are they talking about: a TV program, a book, or a movie?
   A: How'd you like it?
   B: Oh, I didn't want to put it down. It was a wonderful story, and really well written.
   A: Yeah, she's one of my favorite authors.
   – What are they talking about: a TV program, a book, or a movie?*
   A book.
2 What are they talking about: an advertisement, a restaurant, or a TV program?
   A: What do you think of this one?
   B: Well, it's clever, that's for sure. It'll probably help sell a lot of them.
   A: Yeah, it really caught my eye.
   – What are they talking about: an advertisement, a restaurant, or a TV program?*
An advertisement.

3 What are they talking about: a school, a supermarket, or a shopping center?
   A: Hey, it's really nice here.
   B: Yeah. And there's plenty of parking.
   A: Mm-hmm, and also a lot of nice places to eat. Oh look – this place is having a sale! Let's go in.
   – What are they talking about: a school, a supermarket, or a shopping center?*
   A shopping center.
4 What are they talking about: an advertisement, a TV program, or a book?
   A: Did you see it last night?
   B: No. You know I really love it – the acting's great and it's really well done, but it's on too late at night.
   A: I know what you mean. I tape it on my VCR.
   B: Hey, that's a good idea.
   – What are they talking about: an advertisement, a TV program, or a book?*
   A TV program.
5 What are they talking about: a school, a shopping center, or a hotel?
   A: Let me show you around.
   B: OK.
   A: You'll see that all the rooms here have a nice view and are quite big.
   B: Oh yes, they're lovely.
   A: They each have a bathroom and two beds.
   B: Mm-hmm. And what other facilities do you have?
   A: We have a swimming pool and two restaurants.
   – What are they talking about: a school, a shopping center, or a hotel?*
   A hotel.

Unit 15 It's a matter of opinion

Unit 15, Exercise 1

[*Note:* This conversation is on page 94 of the Student's Book.]

Listen to this conversation.

A: How was your vacation?
B: It was OK, but every time I lit up a cigarette, someone asked me to stop smoking. I'm getting sick of all these restrictions! I think we should be able to smoke wherever we like in public.
A: Well, I don't know. Non-smokers have their rights, too, you know. I hate breathing other people's smoke.
B: Mmm. Maybe someday there'll be a smokeless cigarette, and then everyone will be happy.

Now listen and repeat each sentence. Ready.

A: How was your vacation?*
B: It was OK, but every time I lit up a cigarette, someone asked me to stop smoking.* I'm getting

sick of all these restrictions!* I think we should
be able to smoke wherever we like in public.*
A: Well, I don't know.* Non-smokers have their
rights, too, you know.* I hate breathing other
people's smoke.*
B: Mmm. Maybe someday there'll be a smokeless
cigarette, and then everyone will be happy.*

Unit 15, Exercise 2

Repeat each statement and add a tag question, like
this:
– People are friendly around here.*
– People are friendly around here, aren't they?

– Parking is difficult here.*
– Parking is difficult here, isn't it?

Ready.
1 Parking is difficult here.*
Parking is difficult here, isn't it?
2 People drive dangerously here.*
People drive dangerously here, don't they?
3 You can't find cheap housing around here.*
**You can't find cheap housing around here,
can you?**
4 Taxi drivers here are very polite.*
Taxi drivers here are very polite, aren't they?
5 Prices have gone up in the last year.*
**Prices have gone up in the last year, haven't
they?**
6 It's difficult to learn English.*
It's difficult to learn English, isn't it?
7 They should clean the sidewalks around here.*
**They should clean the sidewalks around
here, shouldn't they?**

Unit 15, Exercise 3

Listen to people giving opinions. Agree with each
statement like this:
– People are very friendly here, aren't they?*
– Yes, they are.

– The weather is awful here in the winter, isn't it?*
– Yes, it is.

Ready.
1 People are very friendly here, aren't they?*
Yes, they are.
2 It's expensive to own a car, isn't it?*
Yes, it is.
3 You can't buy much for ten dollars these days, can
you?*
No, you can't.
4 Drivers here are very courteous, aren't they?*
Yes, they are.
5 There aren't any good restaurants around here,
are there?*
No, there aren't.
6 They should really clean up this neighborhood,
shouldn't they?*
Yes, they should.
7 Clothes aren't cheap these days, are they?*
No, they aren't.

Unit 15, Exercise 4

Choose the word that matches the definition you
hear. You will hear the definition two times. Listen
to an example:
– Which word is defined: "criticize" or "contradict"?
– To point out the faults of someone or something. To
point out the faults of someone or something.
– Which word was defined: "criticize" or "contradict"?*
– Criticize.

Ready.
1 Which word is defined: "deny" or "apologize"?
– To say you are sorry for doing something. To say
you are sorry for doing something.
– Which word was defined: "deny" or "apologize"?*
Apologize.
2 Which word is defined: "agree" or "contradict"?
– To give an opposite opinion about something or
someone. To give an opposite opinion about
something or someone.
– Which word was defined: "agree" or
"contradict"?*
Contradict.
3 Which word is defined: "refuse" or "deny"?
– To say that something is not true. To say that
something is not true.
– Which word was defined: "refuse" or "deny"?*
Deny.
4 Which word is defined: "apologize" or "refuse"?
– To say you will not do something that you are
asked to do. To say you will not do something
that you are asked to do.
– Which word was defined: "apologize" or
"refuse"?*
Refuse.
5 Which word is defined: "congratulate" or "advise"?
– To praise someone for success or for a happy
event. To praise someone for success or for a
happy event.
– Which word was defined: "congratulate" or
"advise"?*
Congratulate.

Unit 15, Exercise 5

Listen to people giving opinions. Say "positive" or
"negative." Ready.
1 WOMAN: I think the city has really improved over
the last 20 years. It used to be a very boring
place to live, but nowadays there are lots of
things to do.
– Does she have a positive or negative opinion?*
Positive.
2 MAN: I never watch TV because it's not worth it.
Most of the programs are a real waste of time.
– Does he have a positive or negative opinion?*
Negative.
3 WOMAN: I'm glad I came to this school. The
teachers are helpful and the courses I'm taking
are very useful. I've made a lot of friends here
too.

– Does she have a positive or negative opinion?*
Positive.

4 MAN: I refuse to buy a home computer. Everyone talks about computers these days, but how many people really need one? I mean, most people only use them for playing computer games, so what's the point? I'm perfectly happy with my typewriter.
– Does he have a positive or negative opinion?*
Negative.

5 WOMAN: I think it's cruel to keep animals in a zoo. Most of the time the animals are kept in small cages, and they don't have anything to do. Animals need to have space to run around.
– Does she have a positive or negative opinion?*
Negative.

Unit 15, Exercise 6

Listen to two people giving opinions about things. Do they agree or disagree?

1 A: I think military service is a good idea for both men *and* women. It teaches young people discipline and respect.
   B: Yeah, and it also teaches them how to *kill* people. I think it's better for young people to go to college or get a job. That's a better way to learn discipline.
   – Do they agree or disagree?*
   Disagree.

2 A: I think portable stereos should be banned in public places. I hate having to listen to other people's music when I'm at the beach.
   B: I know what you mean. I hate having to hear rock music in the parks. It certainly would be great if they banned it.
   – Do they agree or disagree?*
   Agree.

3 A: I'm glad they're banning smoking on airplanes. It's really bad for everyone's health.
   B: What's the big deal? As long as there's a separate section for smokers, I think it's OK.
   – Do they agree or disagree?*
   Disagree.

4 A: I don't think tourism is really good for developing countries. It only benefits the people who own hotels and restaurants.
   B: Well, it certainly doesn't benefit the working people. It just creates a few low-paying jobs.
   – Do they agree or disagree?*
   Agree.

5 A: I think people with large families shouldn't have to pay taxes. They can't afford it. It costs a fortune to put kids through school these days.
   B: Well, I don't know. Maybe paying taxes will stop people from having large families. After all, the earth is already overpopulated.
   – Do they agree or disagree?*
   Disagree.